INTERNATIONAL COURT OF JUSTICE WITH SPECIAL REFERENCE TO INTERNATIONAL CRIMINAL COURT

ZAINAB IFTEKHAR KHAN

Made with ♥ on the Notion Press Platform
www.notionpress.com

INTERNATIONAL COURT OF JUSTICE

WITH SPECIAL REFERENCE TO INTERNATIONAL CRIMINAL COURT

ZAINAB IFTIKHAR KHAN

ACKNOWLEDGEMET

Any errors or omissions contained in this study are my sole responsibility. If the study has any merit, however, it is due to the assistance that I have received from many individuals. My supervisor, Professor MRS SHOVA DEVI greatly helped, encouraged, and taught me at every stage of this research. She has been an invaluable source of excellent advice that I could access whenever and wherever I needed it; I thank her for her patience, tolerance, and encouragement in the course of this dissertation... I also thank her for her continuing support and useful comments on my thesis.

Besides her, several other individuals within and outside, AMITY LAW SCHOOL have provided me with unforgettable support.

I would also like to thank Professor J.P.YADAV the Head of the Law Department for their excellence of character and understanding of my situation, their kindness, and support. Moreover, and foremost, I give thanks to my God for opening up the opportunity to expand my horizons, learn new ways of living and spend my time seeking knowledge; I wish to continue in this way for the rest of my life.

ABSTRACT

This thesis takes its starting point from the need for a comprehensive approach towards justice following atrocities, and where not only the states in which the crimes were committed have a role to play. The thesis discusses atrocity crime (genocide, crimes against humanity, and war crimes) prosecution, and reparations procedures concerning individuals as two appropriate courses of action, through which non-territorial states may contribute to atrocity prevention and justice for the victims of atrocities. The analysis addresses whether, under international law, non-territorial states are allowed to, required to, or prohibited from facilitating prosecution and reparations procedures and includes an assessment of the extent to which international law relating to reparations fails to correspond to that applicable to prosecution. The implications of the lack of correspondence are analyzed in light of the historical connection and separation of the two courses of action, the procedural and substantive legal overlaps between prosecution and reparations, and the underlying aims and functions of prosecution and reparations. The study covers a wide spectrum of international legal sources, most of them to be found in human rights law, humanitarian law, and international criminal law.

The study shows that while non-territorial states are included in both conventional and customary law as regards the prosecution of atrocity crimes, the same cannot be about to reparations procedures. This serious deficit and inconsistency in international law is explained by the framing of reparations, but not prosecution, as a matter concerning victims and human rights, thereby leaving the enforcement of the rules to the discretion of each state. Reparation is also considered a private matter and as such falls outside the scope of the far-reaching obligations regarding prosecution. The study suggests taking further the responsibilities of non-territorial states in about city crimes. Most urgently, measures should be considered that bring the Legal space for reparations procedures into line with that for prosecution in, for instance, future discussions by human rights treaty-monitoring bodies and in the drafting of new international victims' rights, atrocity crimes, or, civil procedure instruments.

Table of Contents

List of Abbreviations

ACCG *Allied Control Council for Germany*

ACHPR *African Charter on Human and Peoples' Rights*

ACHR *American Convention on Human Rights*

ASP *Assembly of States Parties*

AU *African Union*

Cap *Chapter*

CAR *Central African Republic*

CICC *Coalition for the International Criminal Court*

CIPEV *Commission for the Investigation of Post-Election Violence*

DRC *Democratic Republic of Congo*

Doc *Document*

Ed(s) *Editor(s)*

Edn *Edition*

ECCC *Extraordinary Chambers of the Courts of Cambodia*

ECHR *European Convention for the Protection of Human Rights and Fundamental Freedoms*

ECtHR *European Court of Human Rights*

EU *European Union*

GCG *Grand Coalition Government*

GoK *Government of Kenya*

GoS *Government of Sudan*

GoSS *Government of South Sudan*

GoU *Government of Uganda*

IACtHR *Inter-American Court on Human Rights*

ICC *International Criminal Court*

ICCPR *International Covenant on Civil and Political Rights*

ICESCR *International Covenant on Economic, Social, and Cultural Rights*

ICJ *International Court of Justice*

ICTR *International Criminal Tribunal for Rwanda*

ICTY *International Criminal Tribunal for the former Yugoslavia*

IHL *International Humanitarian Law*

IHRL *International Human Rights Law*

ILM *International Legal Materials*

IMT *International Military Tribunal at Nuremberg*

IMTFE *International Military Tribunal for the Far East at Tokyo*

KNDR *Kenya National Dialogue and Reconciliation*

LRA *Lord's Resistance Army*

OAS *Organization of American States*

OAU *Organization for African Unity*

ODM *Orange Democratic Movement*

OTP *Office of the Prosecutor*

OPCV *Office of the Public Counsel for Victims*

Para *Paragraph*

PCIJ *Permanent Court of International Justice*

PNU *Party of National Unity*

PrepCom *Preparatory Committee on the Establishment of an International Criminal Court*

PTC *Pre-Trial Chamber of the International Criminal Court*

RPE *Rules of Procedure and Evidence*

SCAP *Supreme Commander for the Allied Powers*

SCSL *Special Court for Sierra Leone*

SPLM/A *Sudan Peoples' Liberation Movement/Army*

TJRC *Truth, Justice, and Reconciliation Commission*

UK *United Kingdom*

UN *United Nations*

UNGA/GA *United Nations General Assembly*

UNHRC *United Nations Human Rights Council*

UNSC /SC *United Nations Security Council*

UNTS *United Nations Treaty Series*

UPDF *Uganda People's Defense Forces*

USA *United States of America*

WWII *World War II*

1. CHAPTER I

International Cooperation with the International Criminal Court

1.1 INTRODUCTION

International cooperation and judicial assistance in criminal matters are the subjects of Part IX of the Rome Statute establishing the International Criminal Court ("Rome Statute").1 This Part IX of the Rome Statute represents a novelty in its provisions concerning international cooperation and judicial assistance in criminal matters with respect to the obligations therein for States Parties. This is in marked *contrast* to the cooperation and judicial assistance in criminal matters before the International Criminal Tribunals for the former Yugoslavia and Rwanda ("*ad hoc* Tribunals") as well as inter-State cooperation on criminal matters.

The International Criminal Court ("Court") is not endowed with police or military forces authorized and empowered to apprehend suspects or to gather evidence. For these tasks, the Court depends, as the two *ad hoc* tribunals do, on the cooperation of existing national criminal justice systems.2 The regime of cooperation of the *ad hoc* tribunals and the Court bear noteworthy distinctions defined by the way these international institutions were established. This Chapter will reflect on the cooperation regime at the *ad hoc* Tribunals as well as the cooperation regime under the Rome Statute.

The *ad hoc* Tribunals were formed pursuant to Chapter VII actions of the United Nations Security Council.3 Article 25 of the Charter of the United Nations imposes a duty on all Member States '*to accept and carry out the decisions of the Security Council in accordance with the Charter.*'4 All States are therefore obligated to

[1]

cooperate with the *ad hoc* Tribunals as an obligation *erga omnes*.5 In addition to this, Article 103 of the Charter provides that:

'...in the event of a conflict between the obligations of the Members of the United Nations under the present Charter and their obligations under any other international agreement, their obligations under the present Charter shall prevail.'

In essence, nothing under international law or treaties can hinder the cooperation between the *ad hoc* Tribunals and the Member States of the United Nations.

The regime of cooperation under the Rome Statute is governed by a different set of rules. The Rome Statute, itself being a creature of a treaty by States, is limited to the rules of international law concerning treaties.6 With respect to Part IX of the Rome Statute ("Part IX"), obligations to cooperate and assist the Court are limited to States that are party to the Rome Statute.7 Only in limited cases where situations are referred to the Court by the Security Council,8 and it is arguable whether the drafters of Part IX envisaged this, may non-States Parties be said to have a duty to cooperate with the Court.

[2]

Whereas provisions in Part IX were agreed upon by the negotiators of the Rome Statute, the practical aspects of its application present a challenge to practitioners of international criminal law. The novelty of the treaty obligations, in as much as it marks a milestone in the development of international criminal law presents a a significant challenge for its application.

Traditionally, the sources of international law have been listed under Article 38 (1) of the Statute of the International Court of Justice as, i) international conventions, whether general or particular, establishing rules expressly recognized by the contesting States; ii) international custom, as evidence of a general practice accepted as law; iii) the general principles of law recognized by civilized nations; and iv) subject to the provisions of Article 59, judicial decisions, and the teachings of the most highly qualified publicists of the various nations, as subsidiary means for the determination of rules of law.

Commentators have argued whether the list of sources appears in a hierarchy as to their application. The challenge with respect to the application of Part IX is whether non-States Parties to the Rome Statute can, notwithstanding their right not to be a party, be compelled to cooperate with the Court owing to the *customary international law* obligation for all States to repress, find and punish persons alleged to have committed the crimes within the jurisdiction of the Court - war crimes, crimes against humanity, and genocide (core crimes). This is particularly challenging where persons suspected of committing these core crimes are nationals of non-States Parties. With respect to States Parties to the Rome Statute, several questions pertaining to cooperation exist, *inter alia* Chapter II will discuss some of the nuances pertaining to the Court's Pre-Trial and Appeals Chambers' views on complementarity.

Part IX provides for the arrest and surrender of persons to the Court. These provisions have been greatly influenced by the experience of the *ad hoc* Tribunals.9 With this being key to the functioning of the Court, there is a need to ensure that the process of arrest and surrender conform to the obligations of States to ensure the protection of human rights of the persons being surrendered to the Court. Questions to consider include: what effect does the infringement of his or her human rights during arrest and surrender to the Court have to the trial of the accused person and whether there are circumstances, where the violations of the rights of the accused, would be so grave as to lead to an acquittal or mitigated sentence. Trial Chamber I in the *Decision on Sentence Pursuant to Article 76 of the Statute* in *Prosecutor v. Thomas Lubanga Dyilo* considered the cooperation of the accused with the Court despite onerous circumstances presented by the former Prosecutor Mr. Louis Moreno-Ocampo, including failure to comply with evidence disclosure requirements ordered by the Chamber and infringement of the accused's right to a fair trial.10 With respect to the above, further questions to address include: what the effect is of amnesties and immunities, if at all; and what effect do they have on the arrest and surrender of an accused and the extent of cooperation between States and the Court. The rich

[3]

[4][5] experience and lessons that can be gleaned from the *ad hoc* Tribunals and other special tribunals such as the Special Court for Sierra Leone ("SCSL") and the Extraordinary Chambers of the Courts of Cambodia ("ECCC") can (although not conclusively) shed light on both the procedural and substantive questions raised above. Chapter III will reflect on these issues in some detail.

Finally, it is incontrovertible that the Court will and does depend on the cooperation of States11 to be able to arrest persons alleged to have committed crimes within the jurisdiction of the Court as provided by the Rome Statute, transfer these persons to the the seat of the Court, perform searches and seizures in the territory of States if individuals refuse to cooperate, or compel reluctant witnesses to appear before the Court.12 Without a mechanism of enforcement, the Court's survival and scope of influence is severely challenged despite the elaborate provisions in Part IX. The question remains: what means of enforcement does the Court have for its survival, or is it the proverbial 'giant without arms and legs' who 'needs artificial limbs to walk and work.'13 The opportunities and challenges of the Court's enforcement mechanisms will be discussed in Chapter IV.

1.2 Legal framework for cooperation among States in criminal matters

[6] Cooperation among States in criminal matters exists in the form of mutual legal assistance between States. This form of collaboration between States is based on respect for the sovereignty of States. Jurisdiction is an attribute of a State's sovereignty.14 It is trite law that there are jurisdictional limits for courts concerning criminal matters. The criminal jurisdiction of States is primarily exercised on a territorial basis. This means that jurisdiction is primarily limited to crimes that occur in a State's territory and by its nationals under the active personality principle.15 The extraterritoriality of criminal jurisdiction exercised by any State depends on the cooperation among States to apprehend individuals who are nationals of a requested State but have committed crimes in the requesting State or who are nationals of the requesting State but resident – in hiding or otherwise – in the requested State. The rationale is that where a crime has been committed, the perpetrator of the crime must not escape trial by virtue of territorial jurisdictional limitation. This form of cooperation by States can be described as *horizontal* in that the requesting and requested States are considered at par in the fight against impunity for crimes committed regardless of where they were committed.

The framework of inter-State of horizontal cooperation relies to a large extent on the law of extraditions. In addition to there being an explicit and written extradition treaty between States, there are two other requirements with respect to successful extraditions under international law. The first is the *double criminality rule*, which States that the crime that the accused person is alleged to have committed must be a crime prohibited by law in both the requesting and requested State. The second is that the accused person cannot be transferred from a requested State to the requesting State to stand trial for a crime where the law of the requesting state prescribes the death penalty as the penalty for the crime. The case *Mohamed and Another v. President of the Republic of South Africa and Others* before the Constitutional Court of South Africa highlights these requirements and particularly the second condition above mentioned for lawful extradition of a suspect from one jurisdiction to another.16 The Constitutional Court ruled that the South African government may not extradite a The suspect may face the death penalty without seeking assurance from the receiving country in this case, the United States of America - that the suspect will not be sentenced to death.

A challenge with this particular model of cooperation on criminal matters becomes evident where there is a gap in the laws of the requesting or requested State on the specific crimes that the perpetrator is suspected of committing and the prerogative of legislative entities in any given State to determine what kind of punishment is merited for a particular crime. The debate around the abolition of the death penalty rages on with proponents and opponents not running out of arguments in support and defense of their convictions.

1.3 Cooperation of States with the *ad hoc* Tribunals

16 *Mohamed and Another v. President of the Republic of South Africa and Others* 2001 (3) SA 893 (CC).

[7]As mentioned previously, States have a responsibility for the prosecution of their nationals who are accused of committing war crimes, crimes against humanity, and genocide in their territories. In response to the gross violations of human rights and grave breaches of the Geneva Conventions of 1949 and their Additional Protocols during the Balkans conflict in the early 1990s, the United Nations Security Council ("UNSC") established an international criminal tribunal to deal with war crimes that took place during the conflicts in the Balkans.17 A similar international tribunal was

established by the UNSC regarding the genocide that took place in Rwanda.18

In *Prosecutor v. Timohir Blaškić*, the Appeals Chamber of the ICTY remarked that cooperation in criminal matters between the ICTY and by extension the ICTR and States are 'vertical'.19 The Statutes that created the ICTY and ICTR give primacy of jurisdiction for the crimes within the jurisdiction of these tribunals to the tribunals over the jurisdiction of States. The standard at the time for the prosecution of crimes of an international nature was that individual States had an obligation arising from the Geneva Conventions of 1949 – also a customary international law norm to punish individuals who are suspected of committing serious violations of international humanitarian law (that is war crimes).20 The primacy of jurisdiction lies with the ICTY and ICTR meant that the States of the former Yugoslavia and Rwanda in particular was to arrest and surrender accused persons within their territories to the ICTY and ICTR for trial.

Many of the persons indicted, particularly by the Prosecutor of the ICTR were residents in other countries outside Rwanda. The obligation to cooperate with the ICTR in those cases, arose from specific statutory provisions relating to this. Cooperation by other States for the arrest and surrender of persons indicted by the Prosecutors of the ICTY and the ICTR an obligation arising from obligations by all Member States of the UN to comply with UNSC Resolutions under article 25 of the UN Charter. There are however limitations in this model of cooperation. During the course of the ICTR's mandate, Rwanda asserted its interest in conducting its trials for the *genocidaires* and there were numerous diplomatic interventions to resolve the matter. The ICTR remained with primary jurisdiction over any person alleged to have participated in the 1994 genocide. There have been cases that have since been transferred to Rwanda for adjudication as part of the completion strategy of the ICTR. Other challenges that this model of cooperation has experienced include the harboring of suspects in States that are not willing to acknowledge that the suspects are in their territories. The ICTR indictment for *Felicien Kabuga* who is said to have financed the media house *Radio Television des Milles Collines* and *Kangura* newspaper, which propagated genocide messages in 1994 in Rwanda, remains outstanding. It is widely believed that wealthy businessman is hiding in Kenya under the protection of the government or some influential figures in the country.

[8]1.4 Cooperation by States under the Rome Statute

States have an obligation to cooperate with the Court. Article 86 of the Rome Statute provides that:

'States Parties shall, in accordance with the provisions of this Statute, cooperate fully with the Court in its investigation and prosecution of crimes within the jurisdiction of the Court.'

Wallace argues that under international law, a treaty, although it may be identified as comparable in some degree to a Parliamentary Statute within municipal law, differs from the latter in that it only applies to those States which have expressly agreed to its terms.21 States which have agreed to the terms of the Rome Statute by ratification are bound by the terms of the treaty provisions.22 The process of ratification is recognized as an indication by a State that it is in full agreement with the letter of the law contained in the treaty. Within the spirit of the treaty, a consenting State covenants not to depart from the obligations placed upon it as much as it will seek to enjoy the benefits derived from the treaty's provisions. In the same vein, States that have not ratified the Rome Statute, but have signed the treaty is bound as a matter of practice to the spirit of the treaty.23 Article 125 of the Rome Statute on signature, ratification, acceptance, approval, or accession stipulates that the '*...Statute is subject to ratification, acceptance or approval by signatory States.*' The process of ratification, acceptance, or approval by a State must be preceded by consent through the signing of the Rome Statute by the [9]legitimate authority in any given State. Consent By signing is consequently indicative of a certain measure of the intention by States to be bound by the spirit of the treaty.24

Requests for cooperation from States Parties are made by the Court.25 It is the The primary responsibility of the Court is to make these requests for its efficient working. These requests according to the general provisions for cooperation contained in Article 87 of the Rome Statute are to be made through the States Parties designated diplomatic channels and, in the language, chosen by States at the time of ratification, acceptance, approval, or accession. The Court may elect to use International organizations such as the International Criminal Police Organization and regional organizations to effect its request for cooperation from a State Party.26 The relationship between the Court and inter-State entities is also regulated by the Rome Statutc. Thc working relationship between the United Nations ("UN") and the Court mentioned in Article 2 of the Rome Statute is explicitly substantiated in Part IX of the Rome Statute.27 The UNSC may be called upon to intervene in the case where a State Party and interestingly a State

24 Article 12 of the Vienna Convention on the Law of Treaties provides for the consent to be bound by a treaty expressed by signing. Whereas the provision is clear that this form of consent applies where the the treaty specifically addresses the issue of acceptance of the treaty provisions by the signature the of state

representatives, one can reach a logical conclusion that any state that sends representatives to international conferences where adoption of a treaty happens, such state unless it indicates otherwise during the adoption process, is wholly committed to the terms of the adopted treaty, although the specific obligations contained in the treaty provisions may not apply outside the formal exchange of instruments of ratification.

[10] not party to the Rome Statute fails to cooperate with requests from the Court.28 UNSC Resolution 1593 (2005) with respect to the situation in Darfur, Sudan is an example of action taken by the UNSC in accordance with the Rome Statute.29 In carrying out its responsibility as the primary body mandated to make orders requesting the cooperation of States Parties, the Court:

> '...may take such measures, including measures related to the protection of information, as may be necessary to ensure the safety or physical or psychological well being of any victims, potential witnesses, and their families.' 30

These considerations for the well-being of victims, potential witnesses, and their families – individuals in a system of law concerning nations – in the process of requesting the cooperation of States Parties with the Court are a strong indication of the centrality of this category of persons during the negotiations in Rome for a permanent international criminal court and the aftermath of its establishment. By fate or chance, the drafters of the Rome Statute left an indelible mark protecting these individuals in the international criminal justice system.

[11]

Since the Court has the responsibility to make requests for cooperation from States in accordance with Article 87, there is a case to argue for a State that does not cooperate with the Court for lack of a specific request by the Court for this cooperation. It would be very rare for this sort of situation to exist as the Court constantly reiterates the necessity of State cooperation to fulfill its mandate. It is, however, also possible to interpret this requirement for cooperation to be limited to the State of the nationality of the accused and the territory where the crime was committed. It would be unrealistic to impute the non-cooperation of the States Party outside of the general good faith of being treaty-bound, without the explicit

request to that State Party by the Court for cooperation. It is arguable however in the situation in Darfur, Sudan where there is an outstanding warrant of arrest for the Sudanese President Omar Al Bashir and other high-ranking government officials, that although no specific request had been made by the Court to countries such as Kenya and Chad, their unwillingness or inability to arrest and surrender President Bashir is a reflection of their commitment to cooperating with the Court at the time of Bashir's visits to the respective countries. Both Chad and Kenya are States Parties to the Rome Statute and failed to arrest President Bashir while he was in these countries. When brought to task over her commitment to cooperating with the Court, Kenya has maintained its full commitment to its obligations under the Rome Statute.31 Perhaps to prevent future excuses by States Party to the Rome Statute from their obligation to cooperate with the Court, the request for cooperation by the Court to a State Party must be specific even where
[12]the request is made to the State of the nationality of the accused or the State where the crimes in question were committed. This can avert situations where the State is castigated for not cooperating with the Court, especially where the request for cooperation is either in conflict with other obligations of the State or there are multiple and conflicting requests from different organs of the Court. This would be in line with inter-State cooperation in criminal matters, where the request is specific to a particular matter and directed on a case-by-case basis.

The Court may also make arrangements on an *ad hoc* basis requesting the cooperation of a State not Party to the Rome Statute.32 Prior to Cote d'Ivoire becoming a State Party to the Rome Statute, it entered into an *ad hoc* arrangement with the Court, and it is on this basis that Cote d'Ivoire was able to make a referral of the situation concerning the 2009 post-election violence in that country to the Court. This can be a a strategy that the Court may wish to employ in negotiations with States that are not willing to fully bind themselves to the provisions of the Rome Statute but are willing to join the fight against impunity for international crimes and may be amenable to agreements with the Court on specific issues.

In order for States to cooperate effectively with the Court, Article 88 of the Rome statute explicitly provides that there needs to be systems and procedures existing within States to regulate all forms of cooperation specified by the Rome Statute. It is the duty of each State Party to enact enabling laws and regulations to allow it to fulfill its obligation to cooperate with the Court when called upon to do so.

[13]

The domestication of the Rome Statute presented a challenge to a number of States Parties. African States constitute the largest block of States Parties to the Rome Statute.33 Of the thirty-three States Parties from the continent, only a half have made efforts to domesticate the Rome Statute.34 Some of these State laws only provide for either complementarity or cooperation clauses and are fraught with implementation problems. There is a need to standardize or provide guidance for the process of domestication of the Rome Statute. This will allow for State Parties to make adequate provisions to effectively cooperate with the Court when called upon so to act. There are instances where enacted implementing legislation of the Rome Statute has led to the arrest and surrender of suspects. *Callixte Mbarushimana*, a Rwandan national allegedly linked to one of the rebel groups operating in the Ituri Province, Democratic Republic of Congo ("DRC"), was extradited from France to The Hague in 2010 to face charges of war crimes in the DRC. Although the Court's Pre-Trial Chamber declined to confirm criminal charges brought against him by the Prosecutor, the precedence set will be useful for future Court requests for cooperation to effect arrest warrants.

Article 89 provides that

'The Court may transmit a request for the arrest and surrender of a person...to any State on the territory of which that person may be found and shall request the cooperation of that State in the arrest and surrender of such a person.'

The lexical reading of this provision is that the Court can make requests for arrest and surrender to both States Parties and non-State Parties. This provision purports to empower the Court to take certain actions with respect to States that are not signatories to the Rome Statute. In this case, the Court has the capacity to request a non-State Party to arrest and surrender a person who is suspected of having committed crimes within the jurisdiction of the Court. In keeping with the law of treaties, however, the non-States Parties are not obliged to act on the request thereby buttressing the argument that the international legal system is still based on State sovereignty.35 The article proceeds to qualify that '*States Parties shall, in accordance with the provisions of this Part and the procedure under national law, comply with the requests for arrest and surrender.*'36 On reading this article, one gets the sense that the negotiators at the Rome conference that adopted the Rome Statute were involved in serious considerations of addressing international crimes of war crimes, crimes against humanity, genocide, and aggression. Owing to the heinous nature of these crimes, persons suspected of committing these crimes should not be shielded from arrest and surrender owing to the non-applicability of the Rome Statute to non-State Parties. This idealistic view must however face the *realpolitik* that States are confronted with in their relations with one another.

[14]1.5 Cooperation by African States with the Court

The Court only has jurisdiction over individuals.37Outside of these individuals voluntarily surrendering themselves to the Court pursuant to a summons to appear or a warrant for arrest, the Court has not been endowed with an apparatus enabling it to implement decisions on the territory of States.38 Swart observes that 'in these and other respects, the Court depends on the cooperation of States.'39 It is therefore arguable that an ideal situation where the Court would function in a seamless fashion is where the trigger mechanism for its jurisdiction is a referral by a State Party under Article 14. Four referrals have been made to the Court at the time of this writing. The first concerns Uganda,40 the second concerns the DRC,41 the third is the the situation in the Central African Republic42 and the final situation is concerning Côte d'Ivoire.

37 Article 25 (1) of the Rome Statute (supra) provides that "The Court shall have jurisdiction over natural persons pursuant to this Statute."

38 In terms of Article 58 of the Rome Statute (supra), "*...the Pre-Trial Chamber [of the ICC] shall issue a warrant of arrest for a person.... [after] having examined the application and the evidence or other information submitted by the Prosecutor... [and] it is satisfied that ... [t]here are reasonable grounds to believe that the person has committed a crime within the jurisdiction of the Court and the the arrest of the person appears necessary.*" Alternatively, "*...to seeking a warrant of arrest, the Prosecutor may submit an application requesting that the Pre- Trial Chamber issues a summons for the person to appear...*" and the same shall issue if the Pre-Trial Chamber is satisfied in the same manner as for the issuance of a warrant of arrest and "*...that a summons is sufficient to ensure the person's appearance...*"; See warrants of arrest issued in the situations in Uganda, DRC, CAR, Sudan and Libya; and summonses for the appearance of individuals in the situation in Kenya and Darfur, Sudan.

These four referrals have however not been devoid of controversy surrounding the cooperation between these African governments and the Court. In the situation concerning the DRC, it is widely perceived that following the issuing of warrants for the arrest of five of its nationals, the DRC has not delivered all five suspects to the Court despite having *de facto* and *de jure* control of the entire DRC.43 In the situation concerning Uganda, the Court has issued five warrants for the arrest of the top commanders of the Lord's Resistance Army ("LRA").44

The Uganda Defense's Forces ("UPDF"), which is the armed forces of the The government of Uganda ("GoU") was involved in sustained armed conflict with the LRA in northern Uganda for a period of two decades from 1986. The LRA was driven out of the territory of Uganda by the beginning of 2005 and into South Sudan. By this time, the GoU was rendered incapable of enforcing the warrants of arrest for the five suspects. It was then that the negotiations for peace began in Juba between the GoU and the LRA. Whereas the GoU was in close proximity to some of the LRA commanders, the pre-conditions set for the peace negotiations included the nonenforcement of the warrants of arrest while the commanders attended the talks. It was later in the Juba Peace Talks that the LRA called for the revoking of the warrants of arrest as a condition for the signing of the last document to seal the Juba Peace Agreement. The Court did not revoke the warrants of arrest as demanded by the LRA, forcing the immediate retreat of the LRA to the lawless Garamba National Park in eastern DRC and an end to the Juba Peace Talks. There has also been hue and cry

about the atrocities committed against civilians in Northern Uganda by the UPDF. None of these crimes have been investigated or prosecuted and there has been a fair amount of criticism that the Court has turned a blind eye to these crimes committed by the GoU.

Cooperation with the Court has proved to be very difficult in the two situations – Sudan (Darfur) and Libya - where the Court's jurisdiction has been triggered by a referral by the UNSC in terms of Article 13(b) Rome Statute and acting under Chapter VII of the UN Charter. Both Sudan and Libya are non-States Parties to the Rome Statute. There is little cooperation between these countries and the Court, with Sudan periodically rejected the legitimacy of the Court and Libya claimed its ability to conduct the trials of *Saif Al Islam Gadhafi* and *Mohammed Al Senussi* both of whom have outstanding warrants of arrest from the Court. Since both situations in Libya and Darfur is a referral made by the UNSC acting under Chapter VII of the UN Charter, one would expect that both Sudan and Libya should cooperate with the Court following a Chapter VII decision to which they are bound.[45] A similar obligation of all Member States of the UN to cooperate with the UN *ad hoc* Tribunals – created by decisions of the UNSC acting under Chapter VII of the UN Charter and in conformity with Article 25 of the UN Charter.[46]

The involvement of the UNSC, a political body in the judicial and legal functions of the Court was a matter that was debated at length by the negotiators of the Rome Statute. Whereas prior to the adoption of the Rome Statute, the negotiators of this

The instrument was alive to the tensions between the political and legal objectives of the UNSC and the Court respectively, this tension was revived when the UNSC referred the situation in Darfur, Sudan to the Prosecutor of the Court and the issuing of warrants of arrest by the Pre-Trial Chambers of the Court for the Sudanese President Omar Al-Bashir and other high-ranking Sudanese government officials involved in the peace negotiations between the Government of Sudan ("GoS") and Sudan People's Liberation Movement/Army ("SPLM/A"). It was widely believed that genocide, war crimes, and crimes against humanity had taken place in the situation in Darfur. At the time, the African Union ("AU") had given the mandate to a High Level Panel on Darfur, which made recommendations on how peace, justice and reconciliation could be addressed in Darfur. The AU subsequently endorsed these recommendations and extended the mandate of the former South African President Thabo Mbeki to chair the African Union High-Level Implementation Panel on Sudan, and negotiate the outstanding post-referendum issues between the National Congress Party and SPLM. These negotiations were poised to usher peace to the troubled The situation in Darfur and South Sudan in general. As a result of the warrants of arrest, the GoS pulled out of the peace process thereby negating the gains and efforts made by the AU to restore and build peace in Sudan.

The relationship between the AU and the Court over the past seven years cannot be described in any other terms but as a frosty one. The genesis of the tensions between the two institutions stem from the timings of the arrest warrants in both the situations in Uganda and Sudan. The AU favored a sequencing of interventions favoring the peace processes in these two countries that were embroiled in decades of conflict, while the Court remains interested in the accountability of individuals who bear the The greatest responsibility for the international crimes that have taken place in those two countries. Consequently, the 13th AU Heads of States Summit was held in Sirte, Libya called for all African States Parties to the Rome Statute to desist from cooperating with the Court or arresting the President of Sudan47 for war crimes, crimes against humanity48 and genocide49 with which he has been charged. The AU has reiterated this decision at its 17th session, once again calling its members not to cooperate with the Court50 after the Pre-Trial Chamber of the Court issued warrants for the former President of Libya *Muammar Gadhafi* (now deceased), his son *Saif Al Islam Gadhafi* who served as *de facto* Prime Minister of Libya and *Mohammed Al Senoussi* who served the Gadhafi regime as a high-ranking military and security officer.

These AU decisions run contrary to the obligation of States Parties to the Rome Statute to cooperate with the Court. All thirty-three African States Parties to the Rome The statute has an obligation to arrest any person at large where an arrest warrant has been issued by the Court. Some countries have made declarations in support of the AU's decisions51 while others have called upon the AU Member States to comply

47 "Decides that in view of the fact that the request by the African Union has never been acted upon, the AU Member States shall not cooperate pursuant to the provisions of Article 98 of the Rome Statute of the ICC relating to immunities, for the arrest and surrender of President Omar El Bashir of Sudan." Para 10, Decision on the Meeting of African States Parties to the Rome Statute of the International Criminal Court (ICC), Doc. Assembly/AU/13(XIII)

[17]

[18]with international law.52 Most recently the President of Malawi revoked the government's willingness to host the 2012 AU Summit on the grounds that they would rather forfeit the opportunity to serve as host than invite President Bashir of Sudan. The Minister for Foreign Affairs of Zambia is also on record saying that Bashir "will regret the day that he was born" should he set foot in Zambia.53 Whereas the African Union Summit decisions call for non-cooperation with the Court, there is little traction on that debate by individual African States Parties to the Court. Most of these States are committed to fulfilling their obligations to cooperate as provided in the Rome Statute. Tladi posits that the AU decisions on non-cooperation with the Court 'raise questions about the direction of international law and international law-making from both a normative and institutional perspective'.54 An institutional perspective relates to the relationship between institutions charged with the responsibility to protect on various levels both regionally and internationally. In this case, the AU has a regional mandate given to it by its Member States to protect and promote human rights in the continent. The Court is a treaty-based body whose objective also includes the protection of the rights of individuals relating to the

1. Chapter II

Contextualizing Modern International Criminal Justice: History & Trends

The quest to deliver a system of international criminal justice has its roots in the first half of the twentieth century, following two destructive global conflicts. This would be an era defined by a few realities. The first reality was that humanity's ability to coordinate the worst kind of atrocities imaginable was both increasingly skilled and tangible. The second reality, relating to the international community's response to the first reality, was that some sort of set of international institutions would be required to stop those in control of state power from causing unimaginable carnage. In actualizing that second realization, though, the international community ran into a major roadblock. That major roadblock pertained to the bipolar nature of the international order following World War II; discussions over the future of international institutions as well as their very goals became gridlocked and paralyzed, plagued by the inherent inability of major world powers to compromise on issues with even a remote relationship to their interests. This period will be referred to as "Era I," a time when the need for international criminal instruments and law was agreed upon as imperative but was nonetheless destined for a stillbirth, if any. When considering the sheer carnage of what precipitated its necessity, the gridlock of Era I indicated a failure for international institutions and global stability. The Quest to Keep Global War at Bay The first 50 years of the twentieth century brought bloodshed on a scale never seen before. Twelve of those years were spent on the two world wars, which took the lives of tens of millions, including millions of innocent non-combatants. Over the course of that two world wars, the world witnessed the horrors of aggression, genocide, war crimes, crimes against humanity, chemical war, and nuclear war. Concerned by the increasing lethality of war, the international community attempted to work out a new global paradigm that would prevent the horrors such conflict brought, both in terms of rule-based international organizations and in terms of ideas that would protect innocents from the horrors of war and violence. The first attempt after World War I was the League of Nations, an international organization that would ultimately fail to maintain the delicate peace reached after the war and fail to prevent World War II. The League was active during that time and it made attempts to establish a hierarchy of institutions and norms that would protect non-combatants from being targeted. According to Professor John P. Cerone, the League considered the idea of an international penal court that would be able to try individuals for gross violations of international norms—like war crimes and crimes against humanity—but was unable to pass the initiative through its Council.48 Cerone cites the future "UN Special Rapporteur Richard Alfaro" for an explanation to that decision, who had claimed "that there was no defined notion of international crimes," nor was there any code that such an institution could follow.49 While this attempt was ill-fated and resulted in little progress toward protecting human rights, it revealed that there were people interested in such a venture which later served as an important precedent. The question of international criminal justice through an international penal court would come up once again after World War II, a conflict that demonstrated that any previously established international respect for human rights was, at best, without teeth. This time, the established post-war order—in the form of the United Nations international organization—stuck, allowing for the actual maintenance of post-war peace. Again, international criminal justice was 48 Cerone, "Dynamic Equilibrium": 282. 49 Ibid. 26 attempted, this time in the form of international military tribunals for Axis war criminals, which came to fruition. The tribunals, though, were flawed in that they could be characterized as "victors' justice," applying only to violations committed by members of the Axis states or militaries.50 Note that while these parties' violations were exceptionally heinous, acts committed by Allied powers—such as the firebombing of Dresden and the nuclear bombings of Hiroshima and Nagasaki—would also constitute atrocities against civilians by today's international legal standards. Despite the flaws of the international military tribunals, they too constituted real progress toward a functioning international criminal code and court that would be able to deter heinous abuses of human rights. After the post-war tribunals, international criminal law would finally emerge, but not before several arguments and setbacks whose consequences linger into today's institutions. As influential as those consequences are, it is important to dive deeper into the failings of initial post-war discussions to establish an international criminal or penal court. The Genocide

Convention & an International Criminal Court On December 9 of 1948, the General Assembly adopted the Convention on the Prevention and Punishment of the Crime of Genocide, better known by its shorter name, "the Genocide Convention."51 The Genocide Convention is an international agreement that defines and condemns the crime of genocide, which had been of the darkest atrocities committed against innocent people during World Wars I and II. Although it does not mince words about how serious the issue of genocide is, the convention largely international instruments to enforce the stipulations that ratifying states swear themselves to. The possible major exception here, though, is the Convention's Article VI, which stipulates the following: 50 Ibid., 284. 51 United Nations, "Genocide Convention." 27 "Persons charged with genocide or any of the other acts enumerated in article III shall be tried by a competent tribunal of the state in the territory of which the act was committed, or by such international penal tribunal as may have jurisdiction with respect to those Contracting Parties which shall have accepted its jurisdiction."52 This section of the convention invoked the possibility of a future international criminal court having jurisdiction over the crime of genocide, which was both a significant point of contention in its drafting as well as a significant point of contention in the American consideration of the Convention, which would not come until Senate ratification in 1986.53 It is worth noting that the stipulations of Article VI are, in the words of Benjamin B. Ferencz (the last living prosecutor from Nuremberg) in his 1980 book, the results of rearranging of already-"watered down" language from a draft convention that had the creation of an international penal tribunal in its Article VII.54 Even in the face of a "watered down" suggestion of a future international criminal court to prosecute the crime of genocide, certain important groups in American society disagreed on the domestic implications of certain parts of the Genocide Convention—a factor that spoke largely to domestic opinion shying away from the principles of international criminal justice developed at the United Nations as a whole. In 1950 the Genocide Convention was sent to the U.S. Senate for approval as a treaty. Senate debate on the subject reveals much about tentative American opinion on the matter. Much of this is in relation to the stipulations in Article VI. In a 1950 executive session of the Senate Committee on Foreign Relations, Senator McMahon (D-CT) noted that the American Bar Association had made objections pertaining to "this business about an international court," to

52 Ibid., Article VI. 53 United States Senate, "Treaty Document 81-15 - International Convention on the Prevention and Punishment of the Crime of Genocide," Legislation, Congress.gov, February 19, 1986, https://www.congress.gov/treatydocument/81st-congress/15. 54 Ferencz, An International Criminal Court: 13-15. 28 which the senator responded was "silly" due to the loose wording of Article VI.55 While Sen. McMahon himself was supportive of moving the Convention out of committee, other senators were not, noting how the reputable American Bar Association had found legitimate constitutional issues with the Convention. The concerns that Sen. McMahon invoked were from testimony delivered by Alfred J. Schweppe, who appeared as the Chairman of the Peace and Law Committee of the Bar Association (and, notably, not as a member of the overarching organization)56 before a specialized subcommittee focused on the Genocide Convention earlier in 1950.57 Among the many points against the Convention he made, Mr. Schweppe explained that while he "yield[ed] to no one in [his] opposition to genocide...," the Convention as contemporarily worded provided no "constitutional safeguards and legal rights accorded persons charged with domestic crimes," which would render any act against an American citizen unconstitutional.58 The full position declared by the House of Delegates of the American Bar Association was that "the proposed convention raises important fundamental questions but does not resolve them in a manner consistent with our form of Government."59 Of course, those concerns had to do with the incompatibility of international criminal law as practiced with the inalienable rights American citizens are entitled to. Here, we see that a contingent of American legal minds, keeping in

mind the severity and complexity of the subject matter, nonetheless cited constitutional concerns specifically regarding 55 United States Senate, "Executive Session: International Convention on the Prevention and Punishment of Genocide - Wednesday, September 6, 1950," § Committee on Foreign Relations (1950): 2-5. 56 United States Senate, "The Genocide Convention: Hearings Before a Subcommittee of the Committee on Foreign Relations, United States Senate," § Subcommittee on the International Convention on the Prevention and Punishment of Genocide (1950): 157. 57 Ibid., 156. 58 Ibid., 198. 59 Ibid., 158. 29 the proposition of an international criminal court as grounds for recommendations for the Senate to not ratify the treaty. As it stood, the notion of American involvement in such an [prospective] international criminal system was unacceptable to these individuals, and they would not be alone; multiple others called to testify before the committee similarly expressed constitutional concerns with the Convention. It is important to further contextualize the issues Schweppe referred to in his testimony. If an American military element (or elements) were accused of genocide, then, if a party to the Convention, would be liable under Article VI, regardless of their interpretation of the situation. While genocide is defined by the Convention as an objective concept, an accusing or accused party's prerogative would be to refute the opposing side's claim. For the United States specifically, a state that participated in many military ventures during the twentieth century, it would make sense to stay away from the Convention in the interest of protecting citizens deployed abroad from any vulnerability to prosecution. With this context and documented opposition to a Convention that, again, bore little in the name of teeth, it comes as no surprise that the United States Senate could not ratify it until well after it entered to force. While the United States would go on to entertain the concept of an international criminal court past these hearings on the Genocide Convention, its inability to ratify the Convention for fear of subjecting Americans to international criminal law would foreshadow the dissension to come in post-war negotiations for an international penal court. A Code and a Court All courts need laws or codes from which violations can be codified, and an international criminal court would be no different. Just as with the post-war tribunals, a code would be required. As the notion of international criminal law was quite novel at the time, there were only a handful of precedents from which to work, most notably from the post-war tribunals. Those 30 precedents, in the form of the "principles"60 applied in those tribunals, became the focus of the 1946 General Assembly Resolution, 95 (I), which recognized those principles and requested the consideration and depositing of recommendations for universal principles, or, "an International Criminal Code."61 Such a code would enumerate the possible crimes whose violations could be brought before an international criminal jurisdiction. Despite significant efforts to develop such a code, the international community to that point in time remained unable to codify it.62 There are nuseveralsons why the community was unable to come to any agreement regarding a code—which was drafted several times in the late-1940s into the 1950s63—that was to be based on principles already implemented in ad hoc international prosecutions. Those reasons boil down to long-standing hot-button topics that happened to come at the worst possible time: amid the tensions of the Cold War. By the time the first draft of a code was presented in 1950, "hostilities had erupted in Korea."64 Any enthusiasm that could have been shared between the sovereign states negotiating such a novel international venture "became a causality of war."65 From that point forward, negotiators had to keep in mind the geopolitical realities of the new post-war order. The Cold War between the United States and the U.S.S.R. had, just five years after the end of World War II, created its first far-reaching proxy war. With that war came diplomatic hostility between the two major power blocs; the Soviet Union "denounced" the American rush to aid the South 60 See: footnotes 69 and 70 61 United Nations General Assembly, "95 (I). Affirmation of the Principles of International Law Recognized by the Charter of the Nürnberg Tribunal" (United Nations, December 11, 1946), http://www.un.org/ga/search/view_doc.asp?symbol=A/RES/95(I). 62 Benjamin B. Ferencz, "The

Draft Code of Offences Against the Peace and Security of Mankind," The American Journal of International Law 75, no. 3 (July 1981): 674, https://doi.org/10.2307/2200702. 63 Ibid., 675. 64 Ibid., 674. 65 Ibid., 674. 31 Koreans as "aggression,"66 thus sparking the crime of aggression tinderbox that would bog down negotiations for a code even further. It is also worth noting that the "major powers were busy accusing each other of aggression and related crimes."67 This made the problem of aggression (not to mention the undefined other "related crimes" Ferencz refers to) a multi-sided one, with both sides employing the same language—which the 1950 draft code of offenses would repeatedly try to codify as an international crime in its Article 268—to shame the other. It stands to reason that as far as aggression could theoretically go in a hypothetical international criminal court at that point, neither side would agree to submit themselves to the other's definition. Given that the Cold War would not end until the 1990s (not so coincidentally the same decade as the final establishment of a code of offenses [The Rome Statute of 1998]) and that proxy wars stemming from the larger conflict would continue to crop up, it also stands to reason that any agreement over the crime of aggression would be difficult to come by. Aggression and Draft Codes The issue of aggression is an interesting one; while it seems to be the factor that doomed both an international criminal code and court, it was previously agreed upon. In 1945 an annex to the Charter of the International Military Tribunal (Nuremburg Tribunal) had declared—declared from the U.K., the U.S., France, and the U.S.S.R.—that "waging a war of aggression" constituted a "crime against peace," the first set of crimes enumerated in the annex's Article 6.69 It was defined to better characterize the criminal nature of Axis military activities and, of course, to deter any further potential aggressors. General Assembly Resolution 66 Ferencz, An International Criminal Court: 19. 67 Ferencz, "The Draft Code of Offences Against the Peace and Security of Mankind": 674. 68 International Law Commission, "Text of the Draft Code," in Yearbook of the International Law Commission 1951, vol. 2 (United Nations, 1951): 135. 69 United Nations, "Charter of the International Military Tribunal - Annex to the Agreement for the Prosecution and Punishment of the Major War Criminals of the European Axis ('London Agreement')," Refworld, August 8, 1945: Article 6(a), https://www.refworld.org/docid/3ae6b39614.html. 32 95 (I) had affirmed a desire for a code and Resolution 177 (II) in 1947 directed the newborn International Law Commission (ILC) to derive a code of offenses from the established precedents at the Nuremberg Tribunal. 70 The ILC had drafted a coherent set of Nuremberg Principles in 1950.71 That same language about "waging a war of aggression" was included almost verbatim in Principle VI in the 1950 Nuremberg Principles released by the ILC.72 Also in 1950, the General Assembly declared that "any aggression" would constitute "the gravest of all crimes against peace and security."73 Indeed, there was great interest in what to do about aggression after World War II, and the General Assembly seemed exceptionally committed to the resolving issue—to the point where it directed the ILC to formulate a code of offenses based on premises including the issue. Following this logic through to the conclusion, as aggression was of deep concern in the Nuremberg Principles (and to the General Assembly), so too would it be in any draft for a code put forward by the ILC as per its mandate from the Assembly. Such a contentious issue had real-time implications. After the Soviet Union declared that the United States' decision to intervene in the conflict on Korea on behalf of the south constituted aggression, it lodged an official request with the United Nations to "agree upon a definition of aggression."74 The UN responded with General Assembly Resolution 378 (II), 70 United Nations General Assembly, "95 (I). Affirmation of the Principles of International Law Recognized by the Charter of the Nürnberg Tribunal;" United Nations General Assembly, "177 (II). Formulation of The Principles Recognized in the Charter of the Nürnberg Tribunal and in the Judgment of the Tribunal" (United Nations, November 21, 1947), United Nations Official Documents, http://www.un.org/en/ga/search/view_doc.asp?symbol=A/RES/177(II). 71 International Law Commission, "Principles of International Law Recognized in the Charter of the Nürnberg Tribunal in the gment of the Tribunal: 1950" (United Nations, 1950), http://legal.un.org/ilc/texts/instruments/english/draft_articles/7_1_1950.pdf. 72 Ibid., Principle VI. 73 United Nations General Assembly, "380 (V). Peace through Deeds" (United Nations, November 17, 1950), United Nations Official Documents, http://www.un.org/en/ga/search/view_doc.asp?symbol=A/RES/380(V). 74 Ferencz, An International Criminal Court: 19. 33 section B with a referral of the question to none other than the International Law Commission.75 This made for an exceptionally full platter for the ILC to deal with, having been mandated to deal with the Nuremberg Principles, a code of offenses based on those Principles, and also the issue of aggression (which was also a component of the other two to boot). Given the geopolitical quagmire that was the early-1950s, formulating a code of offenses or International Criminal Code would be difficult. The General Assembly heavily insinuated that these things should have had aggression attached to them; attaining any agreement between rival powers accusing each other of such acts (and more) would have been quite the task. Cerone concurs with the notion that agreement would have been difficult, writing that the issue of aggression was "controversial."76 Indeed, the literature agrees that the issue of aggression was controversial, and its near-mandated inclusion in a code would prove to make the issue of a code equally so. Getting Past Aggression: An Insurmountable Task? While there was a consensus among several United Nations member states that the development of international criminal law (and all aspects therein) was agreeable, there were some disagreements on the subject. Two years after the ILC released the Nuremberg Principles, in early January of 1952, the Sixth Committee met in Paris to discuss an issue the ever-salient issue of defining "aggression" in any international code of offenses. At this meeting, the delegates debated how to define aggression. At times they seemed exasperated. Perhaps in acknowledging the issue of aggression was a contentious one, the French delegate Mr. Chaumont had suggested a way to neutralize the issue by decoupling it from its political 75 United Nations General Assembly, "378 (V). Duties of States in the Event of the Outbreak of Hostilities, Section B." (United Nations, November 17, 1950), United Nations Official Documents, http://www.un.org/en/ga/search/view_doc.asp?symbol=A/RES/378(V). 76 Cerone, "Dynamic Equilibrium": 287. 34 implications and considering it from a strictly legal point of view.77 Mr. Maktos, the American representative, had disagreed with several of Mr. Chaumont's positions, particularly the ones involving the disregarding of political implications when defining aggression, ess advocated that he "had never taken the conservative view" on the subject of international law and had also personally advocated for an international criminal tribunal.78 The debate would sooner or later always boil down to a political one for the Americans, given their previous adversity topic as well as the fact that it would inevitably become a political issue when submitted to the Senate. Such disagreements were, therefore, irreconcilable. While disagreements like the one between Mr. Chaumont and Mr. Maktos often cropped up in discussions in the Sixth Committee, the parties involved—at least until this point in 1952, continued to reaffirm their commitment to working toward a solution that would produce an international criminal legal system. It was apparent, though, that the issue of aggression was a point of substantial disagreement even in the early days of negotiations. Aggression and the Collapse of a Twentieth-Century ICC The two major power blocs in the Cold War could not agree on what exactly aggression constituted. The fact that the Sixth Committee was unable to come up with any real resolution as to the problem of a substantial definition for aggression was in large part due to profound disagreements over what exactly it was. In the United States Senate, for example, the divide between possible opposing definitions of aggression was clear; Senator McCarran (D-NV) on June 25 of 1951 slammed a "Communist International Brigade" for essentially framing the 77 United Nations General Assembly, "Report of the International Law Commission Covering the Work of Its Third Session (A/1858), Including (A) Question of Defining Aggression (Chapter III) (Continued)," § Sixth Committee (1952): Para. 2, 159. 78 Ibid., Para. 12, 161. 35 United States and its allies for engaging in "aggression" on the Korean Peninsula.79 It would stand to reason that the demonization of communism as represented by Sen. McCarran's remarks on aggression (also taking into account that "aggression" was the phrase that the Soviet Union used in condemning U.S. action in Korea)80 would have been unhelpful both for constructive dialogue between the two states and their associated blocs at the United Nations as well as in negotiations as to the definition of the word "aggression" itself. Sen. McCarran sly not the only member of the Senate to employ this kind of rhetoric regarding communism and aggression, indicating that this was a matter above simple party politics. Senator Joseph McCarthy (R-WI) was made infamous for his Red Scare later in the 1950s. On the same day as Sen. McCarran's remarks, Senator Hubert Humphrey (D-MN), the future Vice President and presidential candidate, also made of to "Communist aggression."81 Senator Ives (R-NY reference to a need to defend "against powerful aggression."82 Considering this rhetoric is in the context of the Korean War (and some of it makes explicit mention of communism), it can be deduced that, to a contingent of United States Senators (as well as U.S. allies), aggression could be defined as something similar to how the communists had conducted themselves on the Korean Peninsula. Recall Mr. Maktos' comments regarding the political implications of defining aggression—here, several U.S. Senators exemplify the American representative to the Sixth Committee's reasoning. Defining aggression, as he noted, was inherently political,83 and it stands to reason given the opinions expressed by this bipartisan sampling of U.S. Senators on one specific day in 1951, the U.S. 79 US Congress, "Congressional Record - Senate" (1951): 7018. 80 Ferencz, An International Criminal Court: 19. 81 US Congress, Congressional Record – Senate: 7018. 82 Ibid., 7040. 83 United Nations General Assembly, Report of the International Law Commission covering the work of its third session (A/1858), including: (a) Question of defining aggression (chapter III) (continued): Para. 16, 161. 36 government could not expect to come to any consensus with the international community on "aggression," especially with states aligned with the Soviet Union, and expect positive feedback on the domestic front. This line of reasoning is, further, not without evidence. In 1950, then-Special Rapporteur Jean Spiropolous of the ILC noted in a draft code that disagreements between the Americans and the Soviets resulted in a situation where any attempts to define "the notion of aggression [...] would prove to be a pure waste of time."84 In addition to the obvious reality of substantial differences existing between opposing definitions of "aggression," the international community acknowledged it. Recognizing the impasse on the aggression question, it is important to again invoke an intertwined relationship between the issue and a prospective code of offenses and an international criminal court. In the above-mentioned 52 meeting of the Sixth Committee, the issue of aggression was mentioned as part of the ILC's mandate and therefore intrinsically tied in with the rest of the work that it was doing in preparing a code of offenses.85 Ferencz (1981) notes that "without a definition of aggression the code was incomplete, and without a code, there was no need for a court."86 The issue of aggression was so interwoven with the issue of a code of offenses (due to the General Assembly's mandates to the ILC) that if an international criminal court were created without aggression defined, the code could not be recognized as complete by the members of the Sixth Committee. Indeed, given there could be no substantial agreement as to what aggression constituted, any draft code presented would be incomplete. As Ferencz (1980) notes, Special Rapporteur 84 Jean Spiropolous, "Report by J. Spiropolous, Special Rapporteur," Special Rapporteur Document (International Law Commission, April 26, 1950), Yearbook of the International Law Commission, Vol. II (1950): 262. 85 United Nations General Assembly, Report of the International Law Commission covering the work of its third session (A/1858), including: (a) Question of defining aggression (chapter III) (continued): Para. 4, 159. 86 Ferencz, "The Draft Code of Offences Against the Peace and Security of Mankind": 675. 37 Spiropolous submitted a draft for a Code of Offenses against the Peace and Security of Mankind in the late April of 1950 that included several crimes of aggression "without attempting to define it."87 Obviously, this draft did not accomplish much, as the Sixth

Committee was still arguing over the definition of aggression two years later. While discussions on the subject continued, it was clear that geopolitical realities and irreconcilable differences between major negotiating powers (and power blocs) sealed the fate of discussions as soon as the issue of aggression was debated and affirmed as a deciding factor in the creation of an international criminal code and associated instrument. It comes, then, as no surprise that in 1954 the General Assembly decided to "postpone further consideration of the draft Code of Offenses against the Peace and Security of Mankind" until aggression could be otherwise defined88 as well as any discussions on a possible about issues pertaining to aggression and the draft code (which were tied together) were resolved.89 These decisions, which came in two consecutive resolutions at the December 4, 1954 meeting of the General Assembly, solidified the Assembly's position that a definition of aggression was a prerequisite for a serviceable code of offenses, which in itself was a prerequisite for the establishment of an international criminal court to prosecute violations of that code. With the draft Code of Offenses against the Peace and Security of Mankind consistently including crimes of aggression without defining the word (due to the constraints on doing so), the creation of an international criminal court was, under the circumstances mandated in this era by the General 87 Ferencz, An International Criminal Court: 20. 88 United Nations General Assembly, "897 (IX). Draft Code of Offenses against the Peace and Security of Mankind" (United Nations, December 4, 1954), United Nations Official Documents, http://www.un.org/en/ga/search/view_doc.asp?symbol=A/RES/898(IX). 89 United Nations General Assembly, "898 (IX). International Criminal Jurisdiction" (United Nations, December 14, 1954), United Nations Official Documents, http://www.un.org/en/ga/search/view_doc.asp?symbol=A/RES/898(IX). 38 Assembly, impossible. Even after the Korean War ended, the deadlock did not improve, indicating that these discussions truly were causalities of the increasingly-pervasive Cold War. Once again, in plenary in November of 1957, the General Assembly remarked on its desire to move forward with the question of aggression, which was still undefined—but importantly requested that the Secretary-General at the time "to place the question of defining aggression on the provisional agenda of the General Assembly, not earlier than its fourteenth session," essentially deferring discussions on the issue for two more years.90 This deferring on the aggression conversations is notable, as it in essence deferred discussion of the draft code further back, which was itself again deferred until aggression could be defined in a December 1957 resolution.91 Once more, the question of an international penal or criminal court to deal with those issues was also deferred until the code and aggression could be dealt with in another resolution at that same December 1957 meeting.92 The action taken in 1957 was almost identical to the action taken in 1954. The inability to define aggression led to an infinite loop of futility at the General Assembly, which had made it so that an international criminal legal system—once a highly-sought after post-war project—was reliant on resolving an issue that simply could not be resolved due to aforementioned differences made more salient by the geopolitical context of the discussions. After the 1957 deferrals, though, in contrast with 1954's deferrals, the subject went into a dormant state for decades, with Cerone discussing the development as an "abandonment" 90 United Nations General Assembly, "1181 (XII). Question of Defining Aggression." 91 United Nations General Assembly, "1186 (XII). Drat Code of Offenses against the Peace and Security of Mankind" (United Nations, December 11, 1957), United Nations Official Documents, http://www.un.org/en/ga/search/view_doc.asp?symbol=A/RES/1186(XII). 92 United Nations General Assembly, "1187 (XII) International Criminal Jurisdiction" (United Nations, December 11, 1957), United Nations Official Documents, http://www.un.org/en/ga/search/view_doc.asp?symbol=A/RES/1187(XII). 39 of the initiative.93 Indeed, the conversations were abandoned, not to be revisited until after several decades had passed, and, multiple human rights atrocities, had passed. By the time the General Assembly had indefinitely deferred discussion on the issues in 1957, it was clear that without a definition for aggression, it would neither allow nor breach discussions of a code of offenses or an associated international penal or criminal court. Aggression was, indeed, the deciding factor—and the consequences of the Cold War made a sticky situation even more untenable. The International Criminal Court Today – A Legacy The dream of international criminal justice as imagined after World War II came to fruition in 1998 through the Rome Statute, but, as Chapter III will discuss, the modern International Criminal Court is not without flaws. The issue of "aggression" was included in the Rome Statute, but was effectively punted for several years until a definition was finally agreed upon and include statutes amended text; according to the Coalition for the International Criminal Court (CICC), the ICC has only maintained jurisdiction on the issue of aggression since the entry into force of the amendments since July 17, 2018—less than a year ago.94 In its release, the CICC qualifies the explanation of the recent changes by noting that outside of a UNSC resolution, the ability of the Court to exercise its jurisdiction over the long-debated topic of aggression is conditional upon other complicating factors, including an agreement to the amendments by States Parties to the Rome Statute,95 not to mention those states not involved with the Court at all. After decades of discussion, the establishment of a tangible international criminal code in the Rome Statute, and the establishment of an International Criminal Court 93 Cerone, "Dynamic Equilibrium": 287. 94 Coalition for the International Criminal Court, "Crime of Aggression," Coalition for the International Criminal Court, n.d., http://www.coalitionfortheicc.org/explore/icc-crimes/crime-aggression. 95 Ibid. 40 proper, the international community remained unable to answer the very core questions it set out to solve in the aftermath of World War II. The discussions to create a permanent instrument of international criminal justice in Era I left a legacy. After that period ended and conditions changed, a modern ICC commenced operations in 2002. That instrument, though, lacks the legitimacy and power necessary to enforce standards of international criminal law and deter violations thereof. This opens the door for a whole array of problems for the Court, which all invariably stem from the disagreements that doomed its creation earlier on. Instead of establishing a functional international criminal tribunal as conceived in the wake of the carnage of the first part of the twentieth century, the international community dragged its feet; granted, states worked to hash out a roadmap for such an international instrument but bickered and drew lines in the sand over semantics and irreconcilable definitions of buzzwords. When an instrument finally was established, many of the topics at issue originally came back to the forefront of argument. Many of those original negotiating states refused to even join the new instrument, thereby hurting its legitimacy and guaranteeing the perseverance of impunity. When negotiations to launch an international criminal or penal court began following World War II, it was generally agreed upon that aggression was to be avoided and that human rights abuses were wrong. Constitutional issues and the reality of Cold War international relations got in the way, but aggression was generally singled out and condemned as an outlier in a world aspiring to be peaceful. That era ended when the Berlin Wall fell, and the dream of international criminal law became real. Not long after, though, the conflict between powerful sovereign states and binding international juridical institutions reigned, but to a different tune. Not only do the same issues remain, but also many of today's world leaders now hold a more cavalier attitude 41 toward aggression, as if it ceased to really matter. The law of the jungle, if you will, has begun to reemerge. As the next chapter shows, the consequences of the past present a tight situation for the present and a dire situation for the future. 42 III: (1991 to Present) International Criminal Justice in the Post-Soviet Era the Pre-ICC Emergence of International Criminal Justice When the Soviet Union fell in December of 1991, international power dynamics were shaken to their very core. No longer was there a clear counterbalance to the power of the United States, which in the absence of the Soviet Union enjoyed a far freer international environment in which to navigate. This was "Era II," a period defined by American dominance of the instruments of the international order. The gridlock that had defined Era I evaporated, removing the need for compromise as an obstacle to the institution of international criminal justice. In the absence of a stronger counteracting force, the United States did support the establishment of several instruments of international criminal justice—the first since World War II—through United Nations Security Council resolutions invoking Chapter VII powers. The collapse of the Soviet Union did not indicate the end of the hostilities that plagued the twentieth century. While the proxy conflicts spun off from the Cold War had come to an end, ethnic tensions mounted throughout the world in areas where the uniting force of decaying ideologies was fading and in post-colonial states still struggling with the horrors of their pasts. Violence based on the burning question of capitalism versus communism waned, yet violence of other types prevailed. One particularly bloody series of conflicts came as a direct result of the waning of ideological influence: the Yugoslav Wars. While the events that set these wars into motion were correlated with the collapse of Soviet-style communism in the Russian sphere of influence, they can be better traced back to the death of Josip Broz Tito in 1980. Tito's socialist Yugoslavia, 43 according to Daniel Duncan, was a state constituting several smaller republics, including Slovenia, Croatia, Bosnia-Herzegovina, Serbia, Montenegro, and Macedonia. Diverse to its very core, Yugoslavia was a collection of Slovenes, Croats, Bosniaks, Serbs, Albanians, Montenegrins, Slovaks, Hungarians, and more. This diversity was, further, multi-dimensional; these ethnic demarcations also indicate religious and linguistic boundaries. Duncan along with Shale Horowitz and Min Ye in their analysis of the breakup of Yugoslavia concur that Tito's firm control over central power in the state was the glue that kept these vastly different republics together.96 It was only after Tito's death that fractures upon ethnic lines were revealed. Duncan refers to the post-Tito administration of Yugoslavia as a "decentralized" collection of "nine presidents wielding executive power: one for each republic and autonomous province, plus the head of the League of Communists,"97 while Horowitz and Ye refer to this "collective presidency" as "a unique form of authoritarian federalism."98 This "decentralized" system would serve to further pry open divides between the constituent republics of Yugoslavia and deliver the conditions in which war flourished. Without the cult of Tito and without the unity enjoyed during his rule, the bonds that linked the different Yugoslav republics broke. His state had, according to Duncan, suppressed "all forms of nationalism" so as "to create a Yugoslav identity."99 Instead of a Yugoslavia united around Tito his ideas of a state that transcended the lines dividing it, there remained only a Yugoslavia heavily fractured along those lines. Ethnic nationalism did finally burst through, and 96 Daniel Duncan, "Language Policy, Ethnic Conflict, and Conflict Resolution: Albanian in the Former Yugoslavia," Language Policy 15 (2016): 455, https://doi.org/10.1007/s10993-015-9380-0; Shale Horowitz and Min Ye, "Nationalist and Power-Seeking Leadership Preferences in Ethno-Territorial Conflicts: Theory, a Measurement Framework, and Applications to the Breakup of Yugoslavia," Civil Wars 15, no. 4 (2013): 519, https://doi.org/10.1080/13698249.2013.853422. 97 Duncan, "Language Policy, Ethnic Conflict, and Conflict Resolution": 455. 98 Horowitz and Ye, "Nationalist and Power-Seeking Leadership Preferences in Ethno-Territorial Conflicts": 519. 99 Duncan, "Language Policy, Ethnic Conflict, and Conflict Resolution": 460. 44 several constituent republics seceded. The violence that followed was unthinkable. War crimes, crimes against humanity, and even genocide were committed on grand scales throughout the Balkans as part of targeted campaigns against opposing ethnic groups. "Ethnic cleansing" became a household phrase. In his book on prosecuting international crimes committed in the Balkans, Professor John Hagan lists a staggering number of incidents that qualified as such, including "death camps" at Prijedor, "rape houses and conditions of sexual enslavement in the area of Foca, in the southern part of Bosnia," and the infamous Srebrenica massacre—"the largest massacre in Europe since World War II."100 Just 50 years following the conclusion of that war—a war that involved the murder of millions—genocide had taken place once again. The massacre at Srebrenica killed "approximately seven thousand Bosnian Muslim men and boys."101 Although this specific massacre was among the worst of the atrocities committed in these wars, it was certainly indicative of the horrific human rights abuses that had been taking place across the former Yugoslavia. It was not long after the beginning of the wars in 1991 when the United Nations Security Council, then freed from the ideological deadlock that had defined most of its history, passed Resolution 827 [S/RES/827 (1993)]. The lack of ideological opposition from the Soviet Union along with the support of its successor (the Russian Federation) and China allowed for this landmark resolution. It established the ad hoc International Criminal Tribunal for the former Yugoslavia (ICTY), the first such venture into international criminal law since the post-war tribunals discussed in Chapter II. The resolution gave the ICTY jurisdiction over any alleged violation of international humanitarian law occurring after January 1, 1991,102 and it would 100 John Hagan, Justice in the Balkans: Prosecuting War Crimes in the Hague Tribunal (Chicago: University of Chicago Press, 2003): 13-14, http://ebookcentral.proquest.com/lib/brandeis-ebooks/detail.action?docID=515745. 101 Ibid., 14. 102 United Nations Security Council, United Nations Security Council Resolution 827 (1993) [S/RES/827]. 45 continue to operate until the end of 2017, when its residual functions were absorbed by the Mechanism for International Criminal Tribunals (MICT), a residual body dealing with any further legal action or other activities involving the ICTY or the International Criminal Tribunal for Rwanda (ICTR).103 The ICTY was not a perfect tribunal by any means. Flagrant violations of international humanitarian law continued to occur after its 1993 establishment, including the horrors at Srebrenica. That being the case, the ICTY was more of a reactive tribunal than an institution able to use its prosecutorial powers and jurisdiction in order to deter further violations. It was, however, effective. In his article to The Guardian detailing the closing-down of the ICTY in late December of 2017, Owen Bowcott writes that during 24 years of operation, the Tribunal was able to produce "161 high-profile indictments," including "former Yugoslav president Slobodan Milošević, the Bosnian Serb leader Radovan Karadžić and Gen Ratko Mladic...." 104 These individuals held positions of authority and were directly involved in the planning and executing of human rights abuses during the wars, and the ICTY's ability to get them in the dock to face justice was meaningful. As flawed as the Tribunal was, it is irrefutable that it was able to deliver justice and stem impunity after a prolonged period where, in the absence of this kind of international criminal law, impunity was all but guaranteed. The ICTY was a major stepping stone that showed that international criminal justice could work as the twenty-first century rapidly approached. The importance of the ICTY cannot be overstated. It broke ground for international criminal justice in the post-Cold War world. It provided precedent for the ICTR, which would in 103 Owen Bowcott, "Yugoslavia Tribunal Closes, Leaving a Powerful Legacy of War Crimes Justice," The Guardian, December 20, 2017, sec. Law, https://www.theguardian.com/law/2017/dec/20/former-yugoslavia-warcrimes-tribunal-leaves-powerful-legacy-milosevic-karadzic-mladic. 104 Ibid. 46 a similar fashion goes on to investigate and prosecute alleged violations of international humanitarian law in Rwanda following the genocide of 1994. It, perhaps most importantly, through its successes, facilitated the rise of a more permanent type of tribunal: The modern International Criminal Court. A Real Permanent Tribunal Fails to Deliver Real Results Somewhere along the way, though, the International Criminal Court met the realities of international politics. Even though the factors that prevented the establishment of such an institution in Era I had evaporated, the Court has not been able to receive the kind of universal support necessary to maintain its operations as a tribunal tasked with applying a universal understanding of international humanitarian law. Cerone notes the key discrepancy between the relative successes in establishing international criminal law in Era II and the lack of success that the ICC has had: "The US has tended to support international criminal courts where the US government has (or is perceived by US officials to have) a significant degree of control over the court, or where the possibility of prosecution of US nationals is either expressly precluded or otherwise remote."105 Thanks to its newfound lack of a counterbalance in power on the international stage, the United States was able to mold the ICTY and ICTR to these specifications; neither of these tribunals represented a remote threat to American interests. On the other hand, as the ICC is supposed to apply international criminal justice on an equal and universal level, Cerone's specifications are more in opposition. As a party to the Rome Statute, the United States would not be able to unilaterally control the Court in a way that would guarantee American interests are not risked. It exerts exceptional power at the UNSC and thus over whatever the Council passes, but it would be no more exceptional than any other state at the 105 Cerone, "Dynamic Equilibrium": 277. 47 Assembly of State Parties to the Rome Statute. Domestic politics within the United States makes this issue even more difficult, particularly given the robust military presence that the U.S. maintains all over the world. The domestic position dictates the international position, and thus dictates the American contribution to the international politics that are hurting the International Criminal Court. Due to the consequences of those politics, the Court is failing to meet its own goals; human rights abuses continue in some states unabated. Impunity remains very real, even in states with compromised justice systems that would qualify for ICC intervention; under complementarity (an American inclusion in the Rome Statute), the Court's Office of the Prosecutor (OTP) is supposed to "defer" and not exercise its authority in "states with functioning legal systems."106 Two major issues are at play in this failure. The first issue has to do with situations that it has found success in prosecuting, primarily in Africa; all of the 27 cases opened by an ICC prosecutor have included indictments against Africans.107 This is a profound issue for the Court, and it indicates that it is either ineffective overall or that it is purposefully targeting Africans. The second issue pertains to the first indication: that the ICC does not possess any significant power. It is subject to the whims of states and of the United Nations Security Council (UNSC), particularly in situations dealing with jurisdictional issues and involving state interests. The ICC cannot mandate cooperation on the state-level, nor can it operate outside its own jurisdiction (events that transpired on state party soil or allegedly perpetrated by nationals of a state party)108 without the subject state's referral or UNSC referral109—which is also dependent 106 Philippe Kirsch, "The International Criminal Court: Current Issues and Perspectives," Law and Contemporary Problems 64, no. 1 (2001): 10, https://doi.org/10.2307/1192353. 107 International Criminal Court, "Cases," International Criminal Court, n.d., https://www.icccpi.int/Pages/cases.aspx. 108 International Criminal Court, "Rome Statute": Article 12(2)(a-b). 109 Ibid., Article 13. 48 on state interests. The Court can essentially run over weaker states but is powerless to do anything about violations involving stronger ones. These two major issues culminate in negative perceptions as well as negative realities for the court, complicating its ability to effectively enforce human rights norms. The ICC as a Neo-Colonial Agent of the West the International Criminal Court's record clearly indicates a lopsided focus on Africa, which demonstrates a phenomenon in which it has been able to exercise power but at the same time lose credibility due to that focus. Indeed, all individuals who have ever appeared before the court (or those who have been charged for that matter) are from that continent. It comes as no surprise, then, that many regard the Court as neo-colonial, even though there are several potential situations under preliminary examination that involve non-African states.110 In order to properly demonstrate how such a reputation is damaging for the institution and for human rights, it is necessary to understand why the ICC has conducted its affairs in this way and to underscore the effects that such conduct has on the Court's subjects and onlookers. In order to understand how the International Criminal Court has gotten into this position, it behooves us to discuss the way such an institution is to gain custody of indicted individuals. The Court is extremely limited in that regard, as the Rome Statute mandates in Article 59 that it is the responsibility of a "custodial state" to duly execute an OTP-issued warrant and transfer the arrested subject to the custody of the Court in The Hague.111 Consider this hypothetical: if the ICC issued an arrest warrant for a head of state or a person with otherwise state-backing, why 110 International Criminal Court, "Preliminary Examinations," International Criminal Court, n.d., https://www.icccpi.int/

pages/pe.aspx; A preliminary examination is the first step in the Office of the Prosecutor's investigation of a potential case. If a preliminary examination is not dismissed and provides significant evidence of criminal behavior under the Court's jurisdiction, then it may be given permission by Pre-Trial Chamber on to a second investigative phase where it becomes a "situation." From there, the Prosecutor can choose to indict individual(s) or close the investigation. 111 International Criminal Court, "Rome Statute": Article 59(1,7). 49 should that state surrender them to such an institution? The Rome Statute assumes state parties will act in good faith in arresting and surrendering those under arrest warrant, which is more likely to happen when it is in the interests of the state. For an example of this, let us consider the four convictions decided by the International Criminal Court. Those four cases are the Al-Mahdi Case, the Bemba et al. Case, the Katanga Case, and the Lubanga Case. Al-Mahdi was an individual in Mali involved with a non-state militia associated with Al Qaeda in the Islamic Maghreb.112 Bemba—the leader of a one-time rebel group active in the Central African Republic—and all but one of his cohorts were arrested by European states without relationships to the case.113 The last individual in Bemba's cohort was arrested by the Democratic Republic of the Congo, which was not the subject of that investigation. Katanga was an individual, like Al-Mahdi, involved with a non-state militia in opposition to the Democratic Republic of the Congo, which had authorized the Court to investigate atrocities committed since the ICC came into being in 2002.114 Lastly, Lubanga, like Katanga and Al-Mahdi, was involved in an opposition militia; he was arrested on the same grounds as Lubanga by the Democratic Republic of the Congo and surrendered to the ICC.115 In these examples we can see a clear trend; the arrest and surrendering of individuals to the Court requires cooperation with states, and all of those individuals convicted were not aligned with the governments arresting them. Some of those 112 International Criminal Court, The Prosecutor v. Ahmad Al Faqi Al Mahdi, International Criminal Court (International Criminal Court 2016). 113 International Criminal Court, The Prosecutor v. Jean-Pierre Bemba Gombo, Aimé Kilolo Musamba, Jean-Jacques Mangenda Kabongo, Fidèle Babala Wandu and Narcisse Arido, International Criminal Court (International Criminal Court 2016). 114 International Criminal Court, The Prosecutor v. Germain Katanga, International Criminal Court (International Criminal Court 2014). 115 International Criminal Court, The Prosecutor v. Thomas Lubanga Dyilo, International Criminal Court (International Criminal Court 2012). 50 cooperating governments were in opposition to groups that these convicted individuals were associated with.

3. CHAPTER III

The Rights of the Accused, Victims of International Crimes and Witnesses Appearing Before the Court

3.1 Introduction

3.2 The Rights of the Accused

3.2.1 Right to a fair trial

3.2.2 The Rome Statute and the rights of an accused

3.2.3 Effect of immunities and amnesties on the rights and trial of an accused

3.2.3.1 Official and evidentiary immunities

3.1 INTRODUCTION

This Chapter commences with a section reflecting on the rights of an accused person before the Court. As a precursor to the discussion, the rights of an accused are linked to the right to a fair trial under international human rights law and international humanitarian law and the enforcement of this right at the national, regional, and international levels. The minimum guarantees espoused in this human right are discussed in the light of the process of arrest and surrender of persons to the Court. Questions discussed include: what effect does the infringement of these rights have on the arrest and surrender of a person to the Court and on the trial of the accused person as a whole and whether there are circumstances surrounding violations of the rights of the accused that would be so grave as to call for his or her acquittal, or mitigated sentence? The conduct of the Court Prosecutor in one of the cases is briefly discussed to highlight these issues. The section concludes with an examination of the effect of amnesties and immunities (including official immunities and so-called evidentiary immunities), and their effect on the surrender of accused persons and the subpoena of witnesses.

In the following section, the innovative rights of victims under the Rome Statute system is described. The discussion on the right to participate in legal proceedings is broken down into the different phases of proceedings at the Court: the pre-trial phase; trial phase; appellate phase and other proceedings arising from the investigation and prosecution of a case. In the discussion, actual Court practice in determining victim status and the evaluations of applications to participate in the current situations of the The court is critically examined. Some observations on how the practice can be streamlined in future situations and cases are also made in the interest of oiling the Rome Statute system of justice. The Chapter concludes with an in-depth analysis of the right to reparations for victims of international crimes under the Rome Statute. The right to reparations is influenced by the right to a remedy under traditional public international law and subsequently individualized under international human rights law and international humanitarian law. In this context, case law at the national, regional, and international courts is useful to gain an understanding of the right. Finally, the right to reparations in international criminal law as codified in the Rome statute is analyzed with the assistance of the first case before the Court to establish the principles applicable in realizing the right to reparations to victims of the crimes within the Court's jurisdiction.

3.2 THE RIGHTS OF THE ACCUSED

3.2.1 Right to a fair trial

The right to a fair trial is a crucial guarantee in the efforts to create and maintain standards for human rights at the international level. The guarantee of the inalienable right to a free and fair trial is recognized in a number of international and regional human rights treaties.130 The very existence of this right in these numerous treaties is

an indication of possible tensions between punishing individuals who are perceived to be 'guilty' of committing gross violations of human rights and the strict adherence to an accused's procedural rights in the conduct of his/her trial. Stapleton recognizes this tension between the minimum procedural guarantees of the right to a fair trial and the practical considerations involved in trying individuals accused of grave human rights violations.131 She asks the question of whether it is acceptable to compromise the rights of the accused in order to vindicate victims of the crimes within the jurisdiction of the Court. Stapleton suggests that the Court must guarantee the accused a fair trial and argues for the impermissibility of any derogation.132

What are these minimum guarantees for a fair trial recognized by international law? The concept envisions a trial of an accused person that provides a number of procedural protections as a base standard for conducting the trial. Widely recognized minimum guarantees include the following rights133:

a) All persons shall be equal before courts and tribunals and are entitled to the minimum guarantees to a fair trial in full equality;

b) The tribunal is competent, independent, impartial, and established by law;

c) Everyone charged with a criminal offense shall have the right to be presumed innocent until proven guilty according to law;

d) The accused has the right to be tried in his presence;

e) The accused has the right to defend himself in person or through legal the assistance of their own choosing; if he does not have legal assistance they shall be informed of this right; in any case where the interests of justice so require the accused shall be assigned legal assistance without payment by him if he does not have sufficient means to pay for it;

f) The accused has the right to examine or has examined, the witnesses against him and to obtain the attendance and examination of witnesses against him;

g) The accused has thc right to have the free assistance of an interpreter if he cannot understand or speak the language used in court;

h) The accused has the right not to be compelled to testify against himself or to confess guilt;

i) No one shall be liable to be tried or punished again for an offense for which he has already been finally convicted or acquitted in accordance with the law and the penal procedure of each country;

j) No one shall be held guilty of any criminal offense on account of any act or an omission that did not constitute a criminal offense, under national or international law, at the time when it was committed. Nor shall a heavier penalty be imposed than the one that was applicable at the time when the the criminal offense was committed.

3.2.2 The Rome Statute and the rights of an accused

As mentioned above, the right to a fair trial has developed over the years. This is particularly so in the context of international criminal tribunals and demonstrated by the substantive provisions relating to the right to a fair trial in the Charter of the International Military Tribunal, created by the London Agreement of August 1945 to prosecute individuals after World War II at Nuremberg, as compared to those of the ICTR and ICTY Statutes.134

For its part, the Rome Statute is replete with provisions guaranteeing the rights of the accused as recognized by the international community under major human rights instruments, humanitarian, and/or customary international law. Article 67 of the Rome The statute enunciates the following rights of the accused as a part of the minimum guarantees: the right to be tried without undue delay;135 to be present at the trial;136 to conduct defense and to counsel assigned and paid for by the Court;137 to examine, or have examined, the witnesses against him or her and obtained the attendance and examination of witnesses on his or her behalf under the same conditions as witnesses against him or her;138 to have the assistance of an interpreter;139 and not to be compelled to testify or confess to guilt.140

contain more substantive provisions relating to the rights of the accused.

135 Article 67 (1) (c) Rome Statute, *supra* note 1.

136 Article 67 (1) (d) Rome Statute, *supra* note 1; this right is limited by sub-section (2) where an accused may be removed from the courtroom where his conduct continues to disrupt proceedings. Such an accused will then be placed in a room where he will instruct his counsel using the communication technology provided.

137 Article 67 (1) (d) Rome Statute, *supra* note 1.

138 Article 67 (1) (e) Rome Statute, *supra* note 1

Article 67 of the Rome Statute contains other guarantees to an accused, which one would not find in the standard international human rights treaties such as the right to remain silent 'without such silence being a consideration in the determination of guilt or innocence,'141 the right 'to male an unsworn oral or written statement in his or her defense'142 and the right 'not to have imposed on him or her any reversal of the burden of proof or any onus of rebuttal.'143 Additionally, the Rome Statute provides for the right of the accused to a fair and public hearing;144 to be protected from more than one trial on the same charges;145 and not to be found guilty of conduct which, at the time it took place, was not a crime within the court's jurisdiction.146

The Rome Statute is unequivocal in ensuring that the rights of an accused are upheld. At the investigative stage, the Rome Statute has placed certain mechanisms to ensure that the integrity of the process is maintained. In this respect, Article 54 (1) (c) obliges the Prosecutor in the conduct of investigations 'to fully respect the rights of persons arising under this Statute.' Article 55 substantiates further the rights of persons during an investigation. These provisions are distinct in the field of international criminal law in that the Rome Statute codifies the rights that are available to individuals who may be the subject of pre-trial proceedings before the Court.

3.2.3 Effect of immunities and amnesties on the rights and trial of an accused

139 Article 67 (1) (f) Rome Statute, *supra* note 1.

140 Article 67 (1) (g) Rome Statute, *supra* note 1.

141 Article 67 (1) (g) Rome Statute, *supra* note 1.

142 Article 67 (1) (h) Rome Statute, *supra* note 1.

143 Article 67 (1) (j) Rome Statute, *supra* note 1.

144 Article 64 (2) Rome Statute, *supra* note 1.

145 Article 20 Rome Statute, *supra* note 1 with the exception being where the previous proceedings shielded the person from criminal responsibility or the proceedings was not conducted independently or impartially.

146 Article 22 Rome Statute, *supra* note 1.

At the national level, immunities and amnesties granted to individuals prevents courts of law from exercising jurisdiction over the recipients of these tools. There are various reasons why amnesties and immunities are given to individuals. In the case of immunities, they mostly present themselves as barriers to liability for the government officials and international civil servants from national courts while these officials and civil servants performed their official and sanctioned acts on behalf of the state or international organization that they represent.

Amnesties on the other hand are a tool used in societies that are in transition from gross violations of human rights to democracy and the rule of law. In all cases where amnesties are used, they serve the purpose of 'silencing the guns' of conflict and assisting in the negotiations for a peaceful resolution to the conflict. Uganda, a situation country at the Court where it is reasonably foreseeable that considerations of amnesty may play in the investigation and prosecution of cases, an Amnesty Act was legislated in 2000 with the purpose of ending rebellions in Uganda by encouraging rebels to lay down their arms without fear of prosecution for crimes committed during the fight against the Government of Uganda. The Amnesty Act of Uganda has three main functions: providing amnesty to rebels who renounce rebellion and give up their arms; facilitating an institutionalized resettlement and repatriation process; and providing reintegration support, including skills training for ex-combatants, and promoting reconciliation.147

147 Section 2, Amnesty Act 2000 of the Laws of Uganda.

This section shall reflect on the Rome Statute's provisions relating to the investigations and prosecutions of individuals who may be immune from the Courts jurisdiction or who may be recipients of amnesties concerning crimes within the the subject matter of the Court.

3.2.3.1 Official and evidentiary immunities

Part III of the Rome Statute dealing with the general principles of criminal law is useful in assessing the effects of immunities on an individual alleged to have committed crimes within the jurisdiction of the Court. In this Part III, the Rome statute clarifies instances where the Court will and will not exercise jurisdiction over an individual.148 Most of these provisions are reflective of norms in international law.

Article 26 elucidates the exclusion of jurisdiction by the Court 'over any person under the age of 18 at the time of the alleged commission of a crime. In the situation in the DRC and Uganda, child soldiers were used in the armed conflict that existed in those countries. The reality of the situation is that these child soldiers were mostly forcibly recruited into the groups as the Trial Chamber found in the *Prosecutor v Thomas Lubanga Dyilo*.149

Whereas the Office of the Prosecutor has taken a strategy to investigate and prosecute 'Those who bear the greatest responsibility' for crimes in any given situation, it is unlikely that a person under the age of 18 years would bear this responsibility. Some commentators however mention that there is a lacuna in the Statute on how to deal

148 According to Article 25 (1) Rome Statue, *supra* note 1, the Court only exercises jurisdiction over natural persons.

149 On March 14, 2012, Thomas Lubanga Dyilo was found guilty of the war crime of conscripting child soldiers. See Judgment Pursuant to Article 74 of the Statute in *Prosecutor v Thomas Lubanga Dyilo*, 14 March 2012, ICC-01/04-01/06-2842

with persons who are not children under the age of 15 years as expressed in other international human rights treaties but have yet to attain the age of 18 years at the time when the crimes were committed. *Dominic Ongwen*, one of the LRA commanders still at large with an outstanding warrant of arrest issued by the Court is a case in point. Studies by the Justice and Reconciliation Project, a civil society organization operating in northern Uganda suggest that while Dominic Ongwen was abducted as a child and recruited as a soldier by the LRA, he 'excelled' in his designated duties and was elevated to become a senior commander by the LRA leader Joseph Kony. Dominic Ongwen and others like him may have committed crimes between the ages of 15 and 18 years, for which the Court would not have jurisdiction *strict sense*, yet such an individual may bear criminal responsibility based on national criminal law.

The domestication of the Rome Statute may also present a challenge at the national level in relation to Article 17 where there is (or should exist) the capacity within national criminal justice systems to deal with juvenile cases. Unless cured at the national level, such a gap may undermine efforts in the local fight against impunity for international crimes.

Article 27 provides that:

"This Statute shall apply equally to all persons without any distinction based on official capacity. In particular, official capacity as a Head of State or Government, a member of a government or parliament, an elected representative or a government official shall in no case exempt a person from criminal responsibility under this Statute, nor shall it, in and of itself, constitute a ground for reduction of sentence...Immunities or special procedural rules which may attach to the official capacity of a person, whether under national or international law, shall not bar the Court from exercising its jurisdiction over such a person."

Official capacity as Head of State or Government has been ground to exclude criminal capacity and was supported by diplomatic relations among States150 as well as supported by national laws.151 It is a result of the irrelevance of official capacity at the Court that an arrest warrant was issued against the President of the Sudan Omar Al-Bashir and other government ministers, and summonses to appear issued to the Deputy Prime Minister of Kenya, Uhuru Kenyatta, and other ministers in the Kenyan government. As discussed in Chapter I, these arrest warrants and summonses to appear to have various effects on the cooperation between Sudan, Kenya, and other African States with the Court.

Article 31 of the Rome Statute presents grounds for excluding criminal responsibility and may count as a form of evidentiary immunity. They include: mental illness incapacitating a person from appreciating unlawfulness of an act;152 intoxication which vitiates appreciation of unlawfulness of an act;153 self-defense;154 unlawful act committed under duress or threat of imminent death or serious injury.155 Article 32 of the Rome Statute provides that a mistake of fact or law, which negates *mens rea,* excludes criminal responsibility and as read with Article 33 of the Rome Statute, a

150 Decision by the ICJ in The Case Concerning the Arrest Warrant of 11 April 2000, *DRC v. Belgium* illustrates this.

151 The Constitutions and other national legislations provide that the Head of State or Government shall be liable for civil or criminal charges while they occupy the position.

152 Article 31 (1) (a) Rome Statute, *supra* note 1.

153 Article 31 (1) (b) Rome Statute, *supra* note 1; the exception to this rule is when a person voluntarily gets intoxicated under circumstances that the person knew that as a result of intoxication, he or she would commit an unlawful act.

154 Article 31 (1) (c) Rome Statute, *supra* note 1; the exception also applies to threats to property essential for the survival of people. Interestingly military necessity is not in itself a ground to exclude criminal responsibility.

155 Article 31 (1) (d) Rome Statute, *supra* note 1.

mistake of law only exempts a person from criminal liability where they have received an order from a superior without knowing the order was unlawful.156

3.2.3.2 Amnesties and the Rome Statute

The Rome Statute does not deal with the question of amnesties. Stahn however mentions three instances where the Court may be faced with the issues of amnesties: in the review of a decision of the Prosecutor not to initiate an investigation or prosecution under Article 53 (3); a ruling on admissibility under Articles 18 and 19; and a deferral of investigation or prosecution under Article 16.157 Stahn presents the a scenario where an amnesty is issued by a state where crimes within the Court's jurisdiction is alleged to have taken place. As Article 17 (1) (a) and (b) require an the investigation, which does not necessarily mean a criminal investigation, the possibility of a conditional amnesty combined with a truth and reconciliation the procedure may satisfy the investigation requirement.158 The Appeals Chamber decision on the admissibility challenge by the Government of Kenya however seems to suggest that for purposes of establishing that a State is able to deal with crimes to the exclusion of the Court, the state must demonstrate that there exists national criminal investigations or trials for the same individuals as are being investigated by the Court and for the same conduct in question. The Appeals Chamber rejected the general truth and reconciliation process in Kenya as a possible avenue to deal with the crimes committed during the 2007/2008 post-election violence in that country. In any

156 Article 33 (2) Rome Statute, *supra* note 1, provides that orders to commit the crimes within the Court's jurisdiction remains unlawful.

157 Stahn C, 'Complementarity, Amnesties and Alternative Forms of Justice: Some interpretive guidelines for the International Criminal Court (2005) *Journal of International Criminal Justice*, 695 – 716 [hereinafter Stahn], 695-699

158 Stahn, *supra* note 157, *698*

event, the Truth, Justice, and Reconciliation Act of 2008 provides, in keeping with norms in international law on the question of amnesties, that there shall be no amnesties for war crimes, crimes against humanity, and genocide.159

Amnesties are generally inconsistent with the obligation of States to provide accountability for serious crimes under international law including war crimes, crimes against humanity and genocide.160 If a challenge to the jurisdiction of the Court or admissibility of a case to be raised by any party on account of an amnesty, the Court remains the final arbiter according to Article 19 and as discussed in Chapter II. The Court has not made any pronouncements on the legalities of amnesties for purposes of prosecutions at the Court. Nevertheless, the emerging norm of the the impermissibility of an amnesty for certain crimes, including those for which the Court has jurisdiction, it is reasonable to foresee that any amnesty, conditional or otherwise, granted to a person alleged to have committed a crime within the jurisdiction of the The court, will not exclude such a person from criminal responsibility and accountability before the Court. As to the surrender of the individuals alleged to have committed these crimes or the subpoena of witnesses with evidence that may assist the Court in the determination of innocence or guilt of an accused, states are obliged to cooperate with the Court within the meaning of Part IX and as discussed in Chapter I regardless of the immunities or amnesties that may apply. Article 71 provides for sanctions for persons before the Court, but the complexities of cooperation of reluctant witnesses

159 Section 34 (2) and (3) Truth, Justice, and Reconciliation Act no 6 of 2008 provides:

(2) The Commission may in accordance with this Part, and subject to subsection (3), recommend the grant of conditional amnesty to any person liable to any penalty under any law in Kenya.

(3) Notwithstanding subsection (2), no amnesty may be recommended by the Commission in respect of genocide, crimes against humanity, a gross violation of human rights or an act, omission or offense constituting a gross violation of human rights including extrajudicial execution, enforced disappearance, sexual assault, rape, and torture.

160 Stahn, *supra* note 157, 701

away from the Court are not sufficiently addressed. The practice of the two *ad hoc* Tribunals on how to deal with the complexities of cooperation – often in difficult political environments are useful.161 Nevertheless, the Rome Statute does not support the evaluation of these issues to national courts, but rather to interpretation by the Court judges.

3.3 THE RIGHTS OF VICTIMS OF INTERNATIONAL CRIMES

The Rome Statute has codified the rights of victims of international crimes for the first time in the history of international law. Victims of the core crimes are entitled to the right to participate in legal proceedings before the Court as well as the right to receive reparations. It may be important to first assess how this right of victims of international crimes arose under international law and how the right has developed over the years to the right to participate in legal proceedings and to reparations at the Court.

3.3.1 The right to participate in legal proceedings

The participation of victims of crimes within the jurisdiction of the Court in legal proceedings are said to be one of the major achievements of modern-day international

161 For more on the complexities of cooperation between international criminal tribunals and states, see Peskin V, *International Justice in Rwanda and the Balkans – Virtual Trials and the Struggle for State Cooperation* (2008) Cambridge. See further Decision on assigned counsel application for interview and testimony of Tony Blair and Gerhard Schröder, *Prosecutor v. Milosevic*, Case No. IT-02-54, 9 December 2005 and the earlier decision in Decision on Application for Subpoenas, *Prosecutor v. Krstić*, Case No. IT-98-33-A, 1 July 2003.

criminal justice.162 This status to express "views and concerns" through legal representation had never before been accorded to victims at an international criminal tribunal. The shift in the Rome Statue from provisions purely retributive in nature to incorporating restorative aspects of justice through the inclusion of this right of victims to participate in the proceedings in response to criticisms of the *ad hoc* Tribunals where there was no provision in the ICTR and ICTY Statutes expressly addressing victims.163 In incorporating this right to participate in legal proceedings, the drafters of the Rome Statute were cognizant of this new role that victims would play in dispensing international criminal justice and particularly the right to participate in legal proceedings may give a measure of satisfaction to those who have suffered harm.164

The general principle that victims have a right to participate in proceedings is captured in Article 68 (3) of the Rome Statute. Earlier provisions of the Rome Statute also, specify proceedings in which victims' views must be sought.165 Article 68 (3) provides that:

"Where the personal interests of victims are affected, the Court shall permit their views and concerns to be presented and considered at stages of the proceedings determined to be appropriate by the Court and in a manner which

162 Chung "Victims' Participation at the International Criminal Court: Are concessions of the Court clouding the promise" 2008 6 *Northwestern University Journal of Human Rights* 159-227, 159.

163 Jorda C & de Hemptinne J, *The Status and Role of the Victim, in* THE ROME STATUTE OF THE INTERNATIONAL CRIMINAL COURT: A COMMENTARY, 1387, 1388 (Antonio Cassese et al. eds., 2002) (stating that the Rome Statute "appears to mark a new step forward ... victims are accorded the double status denied to them by the provisions setting up the *ad hoc* Tribunals. First, they are able to take part in the criminal process... Secondly, they are entitled to seek from Court reparations ....").

164 *See* Silvia A. Fernández de Gurmendi, *Definition of Victims and General Principle, in* THE INTERNATIONAL CRIMINAL COURT: ELEMENTS OF CRIMES AND RULES OF PROCEDURE AND EVIDENCE 427, 429 (Roy S. Lee ed., 2001)

165 Under Article 15 Rome Statute, *supra* note 1, victims may be heard when the Prosecutor commences investigations *proprio motu*; under Article 19 Rome Statute *supra* note 1, victims may be heard when questions relating to jurisdiction or admissibility are raised; and under Article 53 Rome Statute, *supra* note 1, as read with Rule 92(2) RPE victims may be heard when the Prosecutor determines not to investigate or prosecute based on the interests of justice.

is not prejudicial to or inconsistent with the rights of the accused and a fair and impartial trial. Such views and concerns may be presented by the legal representatives of the victims where the Court considers it appropriate, in accordance with the Rules of Procedure and Evidence."

Victims can present these views and concerns through their legal representatives and in accordance with the Court's Rules of Procedure and Evidence (RPE). In particular, victims have an absolute right to attend trial proceedings,166 a discretionary right to participate in the questioning of witnesses,167 the right to participate in pre-trial procedure such as investigations168, the right to be heard on matters relating to decisions on reparations169, and to intervene in appeals concerning reparation orders.170 Article 68(3) also curtails victims' right to participate where they would infringe on the rights of the accused. In this sense, there is a balancing of interests among the parties in the proceedings. Lee observes that 'victims do not have the right to become a genuine party to the proceedings, but they do have the right to be represented before the ICC.'171

3.3.1.1 Victims' participation in the phases of proceedings

At the outset, victims of crimes within the jurisdiction of the Court can only participate in proceedings once the Court's jurisdiction has been seized in accordance with Article 12. Participation of these victims in Court proceedings is not automatic.

166 Rule 91 (2) RPE

167 Rule 91 (3) RPE

168 Article 15 (3) Rome Statute, *supra* note 1.

169 Article 75 (3) Rome Statute, *supra* note 1.

170 Article 82(4) Rome Statute, *supra* note 1.

171 Lee 'XI' in The International Criminal Court: Elements of Crimes And Rules Of Procedure And Evidence.

Victims who fall under a situation that is before the Court must fulfill certain requirements to participate in Court proceedings. Rule 89 of the RPE suggests that each victim must prepare an application to the relevant Chamber for the determination of victim status. The interpretation by the judges at the ICC of this right to participate in legal proceedings has however drawn much attention and it is meritorious to reflect on the various interpretations of the right to participate in legal proceedings.

3.3.1.2 Participation at the investigative stage of proceedings

Aldana-Pindell points out that 'the Rome Statute and ICC RPE do not grant victims complete autonomy to make decisions regarding either the initiation of a criminal investigation or how the investigation should proceed before trial.'172 Investigative powers lie squarely on the Prosecutor in accordance with Article 42 of the Rome Statute. What then is the role of victims at the investigative stage of proceedings at the Court? The first decision on this right to participate was issued in January 2006 by the Pre-Trial Chamber in the investigation of crimes in the situation in the DRC and effectively the first interpretation of Article 68 (3) of the Rome Statute.173 The Pre-Trial Chamber, while recognizing that the general right to participate in the investigation stage of proceedings was not expressly granted by the Rome Statute, nevertheless, granted victims the right to participate in the investigative stage of the proceedings. The Chamber found that this participation of victims was "consistent

172 See Aldana-Pindell, 'In vindication of justiciable victims' right to truth and justice for state-sponsored

crimes' 35*Vanderbilt Journal of Transnational Law* 1399-1501, 1429.

173 Situation in the DRC, Situation No. ICC-01/04-101-tEN-Corr, Decision on the Applications for Participation in the Proceedings of VPRS 1, VPRS 2, VPRS 3, VPRS 4, VPRS 5, and VPRS 6, Public Redacted Version, para. 63 (Pre-Trial Chamber I, Jan. 17, 2006) [hereinafter 17 January 2006 DRC Decision].

with the object and purpose of the victim's participation regime established by the drafters of the Statue."174 Article 68(3) therefore imposes an obligation on the Court *vis-à-vis* persons recognized as victims in terms of which they are authorized, irrespective of 'any specific proceedings being conducted in the framework of such an the investigation, to be heard by the Chamber in order to present their views and concerns and to file documents pertaining... [to an] investigation of ... [a] situation'.175 Article 68(3) entails both substantive and procedural elements of the right to participate in that it affords individuals standing to claim their status as victims and to assert their recognized rights.

At the investigative stage, victims known to the Office of the Prosecutor and the Registry may express their views and concerns where a Pre-Trial Chamber adopts measures in relation to the protection of persons and evidence. This includes the protection and privacy of witnesses and victims; preservation of evidence; protection of arrested persons176 or those who have appeared in response to summons; and the protection of national security information.177 Equally, a unique investigative opportunity may arise, which requires immediate security of evidence, thus necessitating the adoption of measures considered essential for a defense trial. Victims may also express their views and concerns during such unique investigative opportunities. Victims, through their legal representatives also participate in the pretrial phase of the confirmation of charges proceedings.

174 17 January 2006 DRC Decision, *supra* note 173, para. 50

175 17 January 2006 DRC Decision, *supra* note 173, para 200-237

176 Victim representation in the situation in Libya is ongoing at the Court although the suspect *Saif Al-Islam* and *Mohammed Al-Senussi* are under arrest in Libyan government custody.

177 Articles 57(3) (c) and Article 54(3) (f) Rome Statute, *supra* note 1, in relation to the duties of the Prosecutor.

Victims in a number of cases before the Court have expressed their views and concerns about the charges that have been brought against suspects who have been arrested or summoned to appear before the Court.178 The concluded confirmation of charges hearings in the two Kenya cases *Prosecutor v. Muthaura, Kenyatta & Ali* and *Prosecutor v. Ruto, Kosgey & Sang* highlighted challenges in victim participation and legal representation at the Court. On several occasions, Victims' Legal Representatives lodged complaints about the lack of access to their clients owing to Either the security situation in Kenya or the lack of adequate funds from the Registry to effectively consult and confer with clients. In both cases, the Victims' Legal Representatives were based outside of Kenya. As a result of these hiccups, the Trial Chamber seized with the matter has recently decided that the victims in the Kenya cases would be represented by local counsel who would interface with the Office for the Public Counsel for Victims. No doubt, effective participation at the pre-trial stage not only sets the tone for the trial stage but also is imperative for the effective exercise of victims' rights in the entire Court process.

Chung notes two major developments following the first decision to grant participatory rights to victims at the investigative stage of proceedings. First, due to the slow processing of hundreds of applications from victims in situations under an investigation by the Court, in the Darfur region of Sudan; the DRC; northern Uganda; and the Central African Republic ("CAR"), there was growing evidence that the system of victims' participation established in the early decisions was failing the very victims it was meant to serve.179

178 Victims were represented in the confirmation charges in the following cases: Kenya, DRC, CAR, Cote d'Ivoire, Darfur

179 Chung, *supra* note 162, 160

Van den Wyngaert supports this critical failing and explains that the process of receiving individual applications from victims, in standard forms plus supporting evidence, which often must be translated into one of the Court's official languages, is a long and cumbersome process.180 These applications are also circulated to the different parties for their observations before a final determination is made by the judges - first to grant victim status and then to confer the right to participate in a proceeding. Moreover, an order issued by a Chamber granting a victim the right to participate in any one stage of the proceedings does not guarantee that they can participate in subsequent stages of the proceedings. Victims are compelled to submit further applications for assessment of their personal interest181 at every stage of proceedings. Van den Wyngaert laments that this process may work in a national proceeding where the number of victims is not as voluminous as at the Court. The case-by-case approach adopted by the Court inevitably delays legal proceedings and may not be sustainable as the number of situations and cases increases.182 This problem, in the practice of the Court, was discussed at the conference in Rome before the adoption of the Rome Statute. Some delegates at the Rome conference mostly having the adversarial model in mind had feared the 'crippling effect' of granting participatory rights to victims beyond their more traditional role as witnesses.183 Chung further notes that two years after this first decision on victims' right to participate in legal proceedings was issued, the second development relates to the Pre-

180 Van den Wyngaert "Victims Before International Criminal Courts: Some views and concerns of an ICC Trial Judge" 2011 44 *Case Western Reserve Journal of International Law* 475-493, 478

181 In the 17 January 2006 DRC Decision, *supra* note 173, the Pre-Trial Chamber's view is that applications by victims will be on a case-by-case basis to determine the impact of the victims' interests.

182 Van den Wyngaert, *supra* note 180, 479-480

183 Mekjian GJ & Varughese MC, 'Hearing the Victims' Voice: Analysis of victims' advocate participation in the trial proceeding of the International Criminal Court' 2005 XVII 1 *Pace University School of Law Journal* 1-49, 19.

The trial Chamber's granting leave for an appeal to determine whether the various

decisions of the Pre Trial-Chambers had correctly interpreted the governing rules to permit them to grant a "procedural status of victim" or theoretical right to participate, during the investigative and pre-trial stages of the proceedings.184 There was an urgent need to clarify how applications for participation in the investigative and pre-trial stages of proceedings are to be dealt with.

3.3.1.3 Participation in the Trial Stage of Proceedings

The trial stage is the most visible platform for victims participating in legal proceedings at the Court. In this stage, victims are not only represented as witnesses called by either the Prosecution or the Defense, but they are considered as a party to the trial proceedings represented by the Counsel of their choice. Concern has been raised that the presence of victims as a party in the trial stage unduly prejudices the accused in that Counsel for Victims may take on the role of *Prosecutor bis*. Musila notes that

> The Prosecutor's and victims' interests do not always converge and the Prosecutors may often be driven by the singular objective of the furtherance of her/his law enforcement function – establishing guilt as efficiently as possible,

184 Chung, *supra* note 162, 161; *See* Situation in Darfur, Sudan, Situation No. ICC-02/05-118, Decision on Request for Leave to Appeal the "Decision on the Requests of the OPCV on the Production of Relevant Supporting Documentation Pursuant to Regulation 86(2) (e) of the Regulations of the Court and on the Disclosure of Exculpatory Materials by the Prosecutor," Public, 7-8 (Pre-Trial Chamber I, Jan. 23, 2008) [hereinafter First Darfur Grant of Appeal]; Situation in the Democratic Republic of the Congo, Situation No. ICC-01/04-438, Decision on Request for Leave to Appeal the "Decision on the Requests of the OPCV on the Production of Relevant Supporting Documentation Pursuant to Regulation 86(2) (e) of the Regulations of the Court and on the Disclosure of Exculpatory Materials by the Prosecutor," Public, 7-8 (Pre-Trial Chamber I, Jan. 23, 2008) [hereinafter First DRC Grant of Appeal].

> a fact that may lead to ignoring issues central to victims' claims and

concerns.185

If the first trial at the Court in the case *Prosecutor v. Thomas Lubanga Dyilo* is anything to go by, the trial judges are astute and have been seen to uphold the rights of the accused to a fair trial.

The trial process in an adversarial system presupposes that the Prosecution will build its case against the accused and discharge the burden of proof. The Defense on its part will make submissions aimed at creating a reasonable doubt that the accused committed the crimes for which s/he is charged. The Court's RPE however has adopted a hybrid version of both the adversarial and inquisitorial system much like the RPE of the ICTR and ICTY. In the Court's context, the inclusion of the expression of victims' views and concerns are akin to the *partie civile* under the French legal system.

How do the trials at the Court run? All parties, including victims' legal representatives, make oral presentations and interventions at the hearing, through written submissions or both. Victims' legal representatives are not silent observers during proceedings and the Pre-Trial Chamber in the situation in the DRC supports this.186 It is true as well that victims' legal representatives are permitted to observe proceedings and make submissions based on their observations.187 Rule 89 RPE directs that victims' legal representatives can make opening and closing statements. It provides in relevant portion:

185 Musila G, Rethinking International Criminal Justice: Restorative justice and the rights of victims at the International Criminal Court, (Berlin, Lap Lambert Academic Publishing) 2011, 153.

186 *Situation in the Democratic Republic of Congo* (*Prosecutor v. Thomas Lubanga Dyilo*) Decision on the Arrangements for Participation of Victims a/001/06, a/002/06, and a/003/06 at the Confirmation Hearing, 22 September 2006 [hereinafter Lubanga Confirmation Hearing] at 6 – the Pre-Trial Chamber confirmed that Victims' Legal Representatives can make opening and closing statements.

187 Rule 91 (2) RPE; *See* written submissions relating to *Lubanga Confirmation Hearing*

"[...] Subject to the provisions of sub-rule 2, the Chamber shall then specify the proceedings and manner in which participation is considered appropriate, which may include making opening and closing statements."

Rule 91(2) provides that:

"A legal representative of a victim shall be entitled to attend and participate in the proceedings in accordance with the terms of the ruling of the Chamber and any modification thereof given under rules 89 and 90. This shall include participation in the hearings unless, in the circumstances of the case, the The chamber concerned is of the view that the representative's interventions should be confined to written observations or submissions. The Prosecutor and the Defense shall be allowed to reply to any oral or written observation by the legal representative for victims."

The RPE supports the role of the legal representative to intervene in the trial proceedings by questioning a witness, an expert, or an accused.188 However, the Trial Chamber reserves the right to regulate the right to question in terms of Rule 91(3) (b) to take into account 'the rights of the accused, interests of witnesses, the need for a fair, impartial and expeditious trial and to give effect to Article 68 paragraph 3', which relates to personal interests of the victims, appropriateness and the defendant's rights. The Appeals Chamber has endorsed the position that Rule 92(5) RPE provides for a mandatory right for victims or their legal representatives to be notified in a timely fashion of all public proceedings and filings before the Court. In the Appeals Chamber's, view, victims will additionally be afforded access to confidential

188 Rule 91(3)(a) RPE

material to the extent that such access does not breach other necessary protective measures if in the view of the Chamber, a victim's interests are materially affected. In the RPE and Chambers' decisions, we see that the Court judges' have ensured that this innovative aspect of legal proceedings that includes a new party – victims – does not prejudice the accused and does not create a *Prosecutor bis* situation. The Trial Chamber remains in control of the interventions of victims' legal representatives.

Victims are permitted to participate in reparations proceedings, which commence at the end of a trial and where an accused has been found guilty of the offenses with which (s) he is charged. Reparations proceedings commence at the Trial Chamber and are subject to appeals. In this regard, Article 82(4) Rome Statute provides that: "Before making an order under this article, the Court may invite and shall take account of representations from or on behalf of the convicted person, victims, other interested persons or interested States."189

Legal representatives are invited to make submissions orally, in writing, or both as the Chamber pleases relating to orders for reparations that it will make.

3.3.1.4 Participation at the appellate stage and other proceedings

Victims are allowed to participate in appellate proceedings where their interests are shown to be affected. The Appeals Chamber in *Prosecutor v Thomas Lubanga Dyilo* agreed with the victims and the Prosecutor that since the Trial Chamber's ruling to

189 Article 82(4) Rome Statute, *supra* note 1.

dismiss charges against the accused based on abuses by the Prosecutor of nondisclosure of exculpatory materials covered by Article 54(3)(e) of the Rome Statute, affected victims' interests in that they could no longer participate in the trial and concomitantly would not be able to request reparations in the case, the victims could then participate in the appellate proceedings and submit their views and concerns about the Prosecutor's motion to appeal.190

Where there is an appeal relating to reparations orders, Rule 91 (4) RPE provides as follows:

"A legal representative of the victim, the convicted person, or a bona fide owner of property adversely affected by an order under Article 75 may appeal against the order for reparations, as provided in the Rules of Procedure and Evidence."

3.3.2 Victims' rights to reparations under international law

Reparations are the embodiment of a society's recognition, remorse, and atonement for harms inflicted.191 To an extent, reparations represent the acknowledgment that the the recipient has experienced some form of harm that there is a need to redress this harm and restore the individual to the place that (s)he was before the harm took place. However, it is clear that in so many instances that it is not possible to fully restore the individual who has gone through the trauma of an event to the state before the event, particularly because restoration is not merely a matter of quantum. This is true in the

190 *Prosecutor v Thomas Lubanga Dyilo*, 'Decision on the Participation of Victims in the Appeal' 6 August 2008, ICC-01/04-01/06 OA 13.

191 Roht-Arriaza N, 'Reparations Decisions and Dilemmas' (2004) 27 *Hastings International and Comparative Law Review,* 157-219 [hereinafter Roht-Arriaza], at 159.

case of killings, torture, rape, and even destruction of personal property, which has sentimental value attached to it. In these cases, reparations are not to be seen as replacement of what was lost because that is not possible as illustrated above, but reparations are aimed at assisting the harmed individual to, in a sense move on with their lives in a positive sense.

There has been a progressively growing legal basis for redressing victims of gross violations of human rights and serious violations of humanitarian law. Reparations have long been a recognized principle of international law and are evidenced in human rights instruments as well as in the decisions of regional human rights and national courts. It has a basis in both tort (delict) and the law governing state responsibility.192

Van Boven describes reparations in human rights, as a generic term representing 'all types of redress, material and non-material, for victims of human rights violations'.193 Reparations can encompass a variety of concepts including damages, redress, compensation, satisfaction, and restitution.194 Each component represents a unique remedy for victims. Compensation refers to the amount of money awarded by a judicial or quasi-judicial body after an assessment of harm suffered. Restitution is a return to the situation before the harm occurred. Rehabilitation refers to the provision of ongoing social, medical, legal, and/or psychological care to victims. Satisfaction refers to broader measures, which may be individual or societal, such as the

192 Roht-Arriaza, *supra* note 193.

193 Van Boven T, 'Study Concerning the right to Restitution, Compensation, and Rehabilitation for Victims of Gross Violations of Human Rights and Fundamental Freedoms' UN Doc E/CN.4/Sub.2/1993/8 of 2 July 1993 [hereinafter Van Boven], para 13.

194 Van Boven, *supra* note 193; See also Saul B 'Compensation for Unlawful Death in International Law: A focus on the Inter-American Court of Human Rights (2004) 19 *American University International Law Review* 523-584, at 541

verification of facts, the search for bodily remains, public apologies, memorialization, institutional reforms and sanctioning of perpetrators.

Reparations can be material (compensation, restitution, and rehabilitation) or moral. Moral reparations can include a range of non-material measures which address the The victims felt need to be heard, for justice, and for measures to avoid repetition of the violating acts such as the removal of those most responsible from positions of power and influence, the disclosure of the facts of a victim's mistreatment or official, public apologies from governments for past violations.195

Before assessing the right to reparations for individuals as is the possibility under the Rome Statute, the following section shall reflect on the evolution of this right in the form of remedies from a state-centric approach based on traditional international law to the individualized approach stemming from the development of human rights treaties.

3.3.2.1 Inter-State remedies

Traditional international law placed States at the center of the law of nations. Remedies at the international level were therefore associated with principles of state responsibility. As stated by the Permanent Court of International Justice ("PCIJ") in the *Chorzow Factory* case, the obligation to make reparation to another State for the breach of an international legal obligation is a fundamental principle of international

195 Roht-Arriaza, *supra* note 191, 159.

law.196 The International Law Commission ("ILC") has codified this principle.197 Some conservative interpretations of international law continue to limit reparations to the inter-state levels. Consequently, aggrieved nationals of any state can only be redressed where their claims are espoused by their state of nationality and the claim is made against another state for the harm caused to the individual.198 However, since World War II (WWII), international law has shifted dramatically, in both theory and practice, towards the protection of individual human rights and as such, international law now guarantees an individual right to reparation.199

3.3.2.2 Remedies under international and regional human rights treaties

The cause of the shift from a State to individual-centric understanding of remedies has been the development of international human rights law. Most human rights treaties concluded since WWII includes a right to a remedy.200 The International Covenant on Civil and Political Rights ("ICCPR"), one of two core human rights treaties, demands that each State Party ensure that any person whose rights or freedoms are violated shall have an effective remedy, notwithstanding that the violation has been committed

196 Chorzow Factory case (Jurisdiction); ICJ, Reparation for Injuries Suffered in the Service of the

United Nations, para.184; The Wall Advisory Opinion.

197 See Draft Articles on Responsibility of States for Internationally Wrongful Acts, Articles 30-31 and 34-37.

198 For an example of a conservative interpretation of international law, Diplomatic protection was first espoused by the International Court of Justice in the *Barcelona Traction* case. See also Final Report of the Special Rapporteur, Mr. M. Cherif Bassiouni: The Right to Restitution, Compensation, and Rehabilitation for Victims of Gross Violations of Human Rights and Fundamental Freedoms UNESCOR, 56th Sess. UN Doc. E/CN.4/2000/62, (January 18, 2000) [hereinafter Bassiouni], at 6.

199 Though the method by which this reparation is achieved is still open to debate. Shelton D, 'Righting Wrongs: Reparations in the Articles of State Responsibility' 96 *American Journal of International Law* (2002), 833-856 [hereinafter Shelton], at 834. See also the Darfur Commission of Inquiry Report, paras. 596-597, which states the universal recognition of the right to an effective remedy, has a bearing on State responsibility. Thus, an offending State now has an international responsibility to make reparations towards the victims of an internationally wrongful act (which includes international crimes such as genocide, crimes against humanity, and war crimes).

200 See also Shelton, *supra* note 199, 843; Bassiouni, *supra* note 198, 7.

by persons acting in an official capacity.201 Furthermore, it states that the claim to a remedy should be determined by a competent authority (judicial, administrative, legislative, or otherwise) imbued with the power to enforce any remedies ordered.202 The right to a remedy has been found to contain both procedural and substantive components.203 Procedurally, the right to remedy broadly entails that the State affords the victim access to justice. This entails the creation of appropriate judicial and administrative mechanisms for addressing claims of rights violations under domestic law.204 Generally speaking, this means that the victim should have their claim heard by an independent and impartial remedial body with the ability to afford adequate redress for the alleged violation.205 Substantively, the United Nations Human Rights

Council ("UNHRC") has stated that the right to an effective remedy requires States to make reparations to individuals whose rights have been violated. Such reparation can include, among other measures, restitution, rehabilitation, and satisfaction (including public apologies, construction of memorials, and the prosecution of human rights violators).206

Remedies are also available for violations of the International Covenant on Economic, Social and Cultural Rights ("ICESCR"). Though the rights guaranteed in this treaty are to be realized progressively,207 the Committee on Economic, Social, and Cultural Rights have stated that it considers the rights contained in the ICESCR to be capable of direct and immediate operation within the domestic legal system of each State

201 Article 2(3) (a) ICCPR.

202 Article 2(3)1(b)-(c) ICCPR.

203 Shelton, *supra* note 199, 839.

204 UNHRC General Comment No. 31, para. 15.

205 Shelton, *supra* note 199, 839.

206 UNHRC General Comment No. 31, para. 16.

207 Article 2(1) ICESCR

Party.208 Furthermore, States have been encouraged to create accessible, timely and effective judicial or administrative remedies for all justiciable ICESCR rights.209

The right to a remedy is also reflected in every regional human rights treaty. For example, the European Convention for the Protection of Human Rights and Fundamental Freedoms ("ECHR") states that "everyone whose rights and freedoms as Outlined in this Convention are violated shall have an effective remedy before a national authority notwithstanding that the violation has been committed by persons acting in an official capacity."210 The American Convention of Human Rights ("ACHR") empowers the Inter-American Court of Human Rights ("IACtHR") to

"Rule, if appropriate, that the consequences of the measure or situation that constituted the breach of such right or freedom be remedied and that fair compensation be paid to the injured party."211 Lastly, the African Charter on Human and People's Rights ("ACHPR") contains provisions ensuring access to justice, the right to adequate compensation in the case of spoliation of resources and enshrining judicial independence.212 The absence of an explicit and general guarantee of a right to an effective remedy has been somewhat addressed by the conclusion of the Protocol to Establish the African Court on Human and People's Rights which empowers the Court to "make appropriate orders to remedy [a] violation, including the payment of fair compensation or reparation."213

208 Committee on Economic, Social and Cultural Rights, General Comment No. 9

209 Shelton, *supra* note 199, 847; ECOSOC, General Comment No. 3; ECOSOC, GC No. 9

210 Article 13, ECHR.

211 Article 63, ACHR.

212 Articles 7, 21(2) and 26 ACHPR

213 Article 27(1) Protocol to the African Charter on Human and Peoples' Rights on the Establishment of an African Court on Human and Peoples' Rights.

A State which fails to protect an individual's human rights commits an independent, further violation if it also denies the victims of those violations an effective remedy. While most scholars seem relatively firm in this opinion, the areas of controversy in this field surround the precise contours of the effective remedy and whether it can be provided through different means. Some international treaties specify particular means by which remedy must be afforded214 while the ICCPR remains relatively open to judicial, administrative, and other methods being used.

3.3.2.3 The UN Basic Principles and Guidelines on Reparations

The right to reparations developed further in 1985 with the conclusion of the United

Nations Declaration of Basic Principles of Justice for Victims of Crime and Abuse of Power (hereinafter Basic Principles of Justice).215 Though focused on domestic crimes, these principles set forth comprehensive standards for a state's obligation to provide reparations to individual victims of crime.216 The principles state that redress should be granted through formal or informal procedures that are expeditious, fair, inexpensive, and accessible. The principles also state that perpetrators should provide reparations directly and that States should establish national reparations funds to compensate in the event of a perpetrator's indigence.217 Lastly, the Basic Principles of Justice state that victims participate in proceedings that affect their personal

214 Convention Against Torture, Art 14 specifies that States Parties are to ensure victims of torture obtain redress and have an enforceable right to fair and adequate compensation. Though it should be noted that even in this case, litigation surrounding the Convention Against Torture has revealed that reparations can still be denied when a claim is brought outside of the State in which the torture took place. See *Al-Adsani v. Kuwait*; *Al-Adsani v. United Kingdom.*

215 *Basic Principles of Justice.*

216 Bassiouni, *supra* note 198, 9.

217 *Basic Principles of Justice,* Annex, A, 8; Annex, A, 4; Annex, A, 5.

interests.218 There is a connection between the Basic Principles of Justice's concern for the victim's dignity and participation and the inclusion of the victim's participation and reparation provisions in the Rome Statute.219

The Basic Principles of Justice helped to lay the foundation for the eventual conclusion of the UN Basic Principles and Guidelines on the Right to a Remedy and Reparations for Victims of Gross Violations of International Human Rights Law and Serious Violations of International Humanitarian Law (UN Basic Principles and Guidelines).220 While not legally binding221, the Basic Principles and Guidelines aim to consolidate and organize existing obligations to as great a degree as possible.

Thus, several prominent voices in international law consider them to be representative of the current status of the right to reparations under international law.222 The Basic Principles and Guidelines state that the right to reparation is part of the State's core obligation to respect, ensure respect and implement international human rights law and international humanitarian law.223 They enshrine three basic rights for victims of international crimes: the right of access to justice, the right to reparation for harm suffered and the right to truth.224 Concerning reparation, any measures provided should be "proportional to the gravity of the violations and the harms suffered" and should be derived from the perpetrator, if possible, with the State providing monetary

218 This encouragement was qualified as the *Basic Principles of Justice* seek to ensure such participation is in line with the rights of the accused and relevant national criminal law and procedure, *Basic Principles of Justice*, Annex, A, 6 (b).

219 Ferstman C, "NGOs and the Role of Victims in International Criminal Justice" Seminar organized by the Forum for International Criminal Justice and Conflict, Monday 2 October 2006

220 Basic Principles and Guidelines on the Right to a Remedy and Reparations for Victims of Gross Violations of International Human Rights Law and Serious Violations of International Humanitarian Law, GA Res., UNGAOR, 60th Sess., UN Doc. A/Res/60/147 (16 December 2005) [hereinafter Basic Principles and Guidelines]

221 Rombouts et al, in De Feyter, 362.

222 Van Boven, in Ferstman et al, 32.

223 Basic Principles and Guidelines, *supra* note 220, Principle I, (1); II (3) (d).

224 Basic Principles and Guidelines, *supra* note 220; Bassiouni, *supra* note 198, 28-34.

compensation when this is not possible.225 Reparations judgments should be enforceable domestically and reparation is deemed to include restitution, compensation, rehabilitation, satisfaction, and guarantees of non-repetition.226 Restitution should seek to "restore the victim to the original situation before the gross violations" occurred.227 Compensation should be provided for any economically assessable damage including, among other things, physical and mental harm, lost economic opportunities, material damages (loss of earnings or earnings potential), moral damages, and costs (medical, psychological, and the like).228 Rehabilitation includes medical, psychological care, and legal and social services.229 Satisfaction measures include the cessation of a continuing violation, verification of facts and public disclosure of the truth, the location of the disappeared, assistance with the recovery, identification, and reburial of bodies in accordance with the victim's family's wishes and cultural practices.230 Moreover, satisfaction also includes various symbolic reparations such as official declarations or judicial decisions restoring the dignity of the victim or their family, public apologies or commemorations, and tributes to the victims.231 Satisfaction also entails longer-term goals, such as the creation and promotion of mechanisms for preventing and monitoring social conflicts and their resolution.232 Lastly, guarantees of non-repetition include, among other things, ensuring that the military is under civilian control, that all judicial proceedings accord with due process, and that judicial independence is ensured.233

225 Basic Principles and Guidelines, *supra* note 220, Principle, IX, (15).

226 Basic Principles and Guidelines, *supra* note 220, Principle, IX, (17-18).

227 Basic Principles and Guidelines, *supra* note 220, Principle IX, (19).

228 Basic Principles and Guidelines, *supra* note 220, Principle IX, (20)

229 Basic Principles and Guidelines, *supra* note 220, Principle, IX, (21)

230 Basic Principles and Guidelines, *supra* note 220, Principle, IX, (22) (a)-(c).

231 Basic Principles and Guidelines, *supra* note 220, Principle IX, (22) (d), (e), (g).

232 Basic Principles and Guidelines, *supra* note 220, Principle, IX, (23) (g).

233 Basic Principles and Guidelines, *supra* note 220, Principle IX, (23), (a)-(c).

3.3.2.4 Remedies under international humanitarian law (IHL)

Though strongly debated, IHL contains elements of a right to a remedy. The 1907 Hague Convention requires that a State which violates its terms pay compensation.234 The Geneva Conventions furthered this protection by formally prohibiting agreements between States which would absolve liability for 'grave breaches' of IHL.235 Furthermore, Additional Protocol I reaffirmed that a party to an international armed conflict that violates its IHL obligations shall, if the case demands, be liable to pay compensation and bear responsibility for the actions of individuals in its armed forces.236

However, despite the seemingly explicit provisions in the IHL treaties above, the existence of an individual right to reparation for violations in IHL is contested.237 Some argue that under IHL, individuals are limited to asking the State of their nationality to espouse a claim for diplomatic protection and assert claims for compensation from the violating State in question. Others, including the International The Committee of the Red Cross argues that the trend of international law is towards the recognition of the individual's right to a remedy and specific reparations in the context of IHL violations.238 For the purposes of this paper, it is enough to note that reparations of some kind (whether requested by a State or an individual) are due to victims of international crimes.

234 Article 3, 1907 Hague Convention.

235 Article 148, Geneva Convention Relative to the Protection of Civilian Persons in Time of War of August 12, 1949.

236 Art. 91, Additional Protocol I.

237 See contra, Bassiouni, *supra* note 198, 9; ICRC Customary IHL Study Rules, 537, 541-546.

238 ICRC CUSTOMARY IHL Study Rules, 537 and discussion of State practice at 541-546.

3.3.2.5 Reparations in practice at the international level

Practice at the international level with regard to giving effect to the right to reparations have, in general, been disappointing. There has been some individual successes, but there has been little actual compensation to victims for violations.239 The UNHRC generally issues general or declaratory decisions and affords States a large margin of appreciation on specific reparation awards.240 Nevertheless, in cases pertaining to the right to life and the prohibition of torture, the UNHRC has expressed the view that States are under a legal obligation to investigate, take actions thereon, bring to justice the persons found responsible, and extend treatment to the victims.241 The UNHRC has also recommended the payment of "adequate" or "appropriate compensation" in recent cases.242 Though underwhelming, the UNHRC's decisions can be conceived as providing victims of human rights abuses a measure of satisfaction and a guarantee against non-repetition.

States have also provided reparations to victims by means of inter-State negotiation. For example, as a result of international negotiation and lobbying, Holocaust victims have been compensated by Germany through a variety of means. Under the German *weidergutmachung* law, individual compensation was given to victims or the State of Israel (if no living survivors). In total, Germany has provided $104 billion to victims of Nazi crimes. It has also provided apologies, restitution of lost property,

239 Sarkin, in De Feyter, 155.

240 Oette, in Ferstman et al, 219.

241 Van Boven, in Ferstman et al, 23.

242 Rombouts et al, in De Feyter, 377 referring to the UNHRC decisions Sminova v. Russia; Perterer v. Austria; Kankanamge v. Sri Lanka. The preference for general recommendations to pay compensation is echoed in the practice of the UN Committee Against Torture. See Oette, in Ferstman et al, 238.

compensatory pensions and other measures aimed to supplement the material compensation provided by legal measures.243

Claims Commissions provide another method for victims to obtain reparations from

States for violations of international law. Through institutions such as the UN Claims Commission and the Ethiopia-Eritrea Claims Commission, victims have been able to gain some measure of reparations.244 Lastly, several international reparations funds, such as the Voluntary Fund for Victims of Torture, have been established to provide compensation to victims. This fund is supported by voluntary donations from States, organizations, and individuals and provide funding to non-governmental organizations that assist torture victims and their families. It is one of the largest United Nations humanitarian funds with a budget of $13 million.245 Other examples of international reparations funds include the UN Voluntary Trust Fund on Contemporary Forms of Slavery, the UN Development Program Trust Fund for Rwanda and the Court's Trust Fund for Victims ("TFV").

3.3.2.6 Reparations in practice at the regional level

243 Bassiouni, *supra* note 198, 10; Shelton, *supra* note 199, 841-844; It should be noted that Germany's practice with respect to the international crimes committed during WWII has not been adopted universally. Japan, for example, has taken a markedly different path. It has staunchly refused to pay individual claims arising out of its WWII actions. It has compensated some States for WWII-related activities (roughly $3.9 billion to the Philippines, Vietnam, Burma, and Indonesia). It has also created a 'Consolation fund' for former 'comfort women' of the Japanese Army. However, compensation claims in the Japanese courts and in the United States court system have failed due to, among other reasons, statutes of limitations and the waivers found in the peace treaties signed after WWII.

244 As of July 2004, the overall amount of compensation made available by the UN Claims Commission was $18 billion; See also Shelton, *supra* note 199, 852; ICRC, CUSTOMARY IHL Study Rules, 542. For information on the Ethiopia-Eritrea Claims Commission, see ICRC, CUSTOMARY IHL Study Rules, 542.

245 See also Bassiouni, *supra* note 198, 34; Roht-Arriaza, *supra* note 191, 175.

As noted above, almost every regional human rights treaty guarantees a right to a remedy (in one form or another). The practice of these regional systems has been very instructive in fleshing out the contours of the right to reparations under international law.

The IACtHR has, arguably, generated the most important jurisprudence on forms of reparations other than, or in addition to, compensation. It has stated consistently that the obligation to provide reparations reflects a rule of customary law246 and has ordered a wide range of innovative measures247 within the traditional categories: restitution,248 compensation,249 rehabilitation,250 and satisfaction251 and guarantees of non-repetition.252 Furthermore, the IACtHR has set up trust funds, appointed experts and kept cases open in order to monitor the implementation of the ordered remedies.253

In contrast, the European Court on Human Rights ("ECtHR") has been very conservative when ordering reparations, limiting its exercise for the most part to

246 Shelton, *supra* note 199, 841.

247 Faúndez Ledesma, The Inter-American System for the Protection of Human Rights: Institutional and procedural aspects / Héctor Faúndez Ledesma. -- 3 ed. -- San José, C.R. :Instituto Interamericano de Derechos Humanos, 2008.

248 The IACtHR has determined that the ideal outcome of a guarantee of "fair and adequate compensation" is full restitution, i.e., the restoration of the status quo ante. However, where this is not possible, compensation is often required. De Greiff, Handbook, 455.

249 Examples of this category of reparation measures include reimbursement of costs and expenses.

250 Examples of this category of reparation measures include medical and psychological treatment.

251 Examples of this category of reparation measures include public apologies or symbolic memorials.

252 In general, reparations measure only benefit the direct victims of the human rights violation that have been recognized as such in the first stages of the procedure before the Inter-American Commission on Human Rights and they are next of kin. However, in some cases, with the aim to address

the causes of violations in order to prevent recurrence the IACtHR, has also specified a range of measures including investigation, prosecution, and punishment of those responsible, legislative and institutional reforms, as well as training as "guarantees of non-repetition". As a result of the compliance of these measures, such judgments have had a wide effect, reaching individuals that have not appeared as applicants before the Court but were suffering the same human rights violation. In this respect, what is noteworthy about these types of measures is that at the same time addressing the problem of limited access to the international system, has also secured in some aspects the effective domestication of the American Convention. See: IACtHR, Case of "The Last Temptation of Christ" (Olmedo-Bustos et al.) v. Chile. Merits, Reparations, and Costs. Judgment of February 5, 2001. Series C No. 73

253 Shelton, *supra* note 199, 841.

monetary reparation. Furthermore, the President of the Court has indicated that just satisfaction254 does not automatically flow from the finding of a violation of the ECHR or its Protocols. Furthermore, the President stated that compensation will be granted only in default of the domestic judicial system to guarantee a full reparation and only "if necessary".255

Finally, the case law of the African Commission on Human and Peoples' Rights shows hesitation in making specific recommendations on awards for compensation or other forms of reparations. Instead, the Commission has preferred to declare a violation and grant the State Party a measure of discretion in terms of the implementation of the remedy.256

3.3.3 The right to reparations under the Rome Statute

As previously mentioned, one of the fundamental contributions of the Rome Statute to the body of international criminal law is the provision of the right to reparations to victims of crimes covered by the Statute.257 There are two key provisions in the Rome Statute pertaining to this right to reparation. Article 75 relates to the right of reparations to victims and Article 79 establishes the Trust Fund for Victims (TFV) for the benefit of victims of crimes within the jurisdiction of the Court and families of such victims. In the relevant portion Article 75 provides that:

254 Article 41, ECHR.

255 President of the ECHR, Practice Direction, Just Satisfaction Claims. 28 March 2007, Available at: http://www.echr.coe.int/NR/rdonlyres/8227A775-CD37-4F51-A4AA-1797004BE394/0/PracticeDirectionsJustSatifactionClaims2007.pdf

256 Oette, in Ferstman et al, 219.

257 Haslam E, 'Victim Participation at the International Criminal Court: A triumph of hope over experience?' in D. McGoldrick, P Rowe & E Donnely, The Permanent International Criminal Court: Legal and Policies Issues (2004) 315-334

The Court shall establish principles relating to reparations to, or in respect of, victims, including restitution, compensation, and rehabilitation... determine the scope and extent of any damage, loss, and injury to, or in respect of, victims and will state the principles on which it is acting. 258

After making a determination as to the award, the Court is empowered to make an order directly against a convicted person specifying appropriate reparations to, or in respect of, victims. The Court may order that such an award is made through the TFV. Rules 94 to 96 RPE set out the procedures for reparations to victims. These rules direct that the Court may invite to the reparations' hearings not only the victims and the convicted person, but also interested persons or interested States whose properties could be affected by the rulings on reparations. Nevertheless, neither the Rome The statute nor the RPE prescribes how these provisions regarding reparations will be implemented.259

3.3.3.1 Decision establishing principles and procedures to be applied to reparations

258 Article 75(1) Rome Statute; *See* Donat-Cattin D, 'Article 68' in Triffterer *Commentary on the Rome Statute of the International Criminal Court: Observer's notes article by article* (1999) 965-1014 for a history of the provision relating to the right to reparations.

259 Henzelin M, Heiskanen V & Mettraux G, 'Reparations to Victims Before the International Criminal Court: Lessons from international mass claims processes' (2006) 17 *Criminal Law Forum* 317-344, at 338 noting that the 'Statute and Rules do not provide...any predetermined mechanisms or procedures for processing reparations claims and implementation of awards'

Trial Chamber I in the case of the *Prosecutor v. Thomas Lubanga Dyilo* established the principles and procedures to be applied to reparations in August 2012.260 This the decision followed the Judgment Pursuant to Article 74 of the Rome Statute in the the same case where the accused *Thomas Lubanga Dyilo* was found guilty of the war crimes that he was charged with – including conscripting or enlisting children under the age of fifteen years into armed forces or groups and using them to participate on the hostilities. This is the first decision by the Court interpreting the right to reparations and sets important benchmarks and foundations in the reparations regime and victimology in international criminal justice.

In terms of the procedure that was followed in the determination of the Court's principles and procedures to be applied to reparations in line with the RPE, the Trial The chamber granted leave for submissions from the following parties before making its final determination on the matter: the Office of the Prosecutor; The defense of the convicted person; Legal Representatives of Victims; the Registry; Office of Public Counsel for Victims; Trust Fund for Victims; and other parties: Women's Initiatives for Gender Justice; International Centre for Transitional Justice, UNICEF, Foundation Congolaise pour la Promotion des Droits humains et la Paix, Avocats sans Frontières and certain other Non-Governmental Organisations.261

In establishing the principles relating to reparations pursuant to Article 75 (1) of the

Rome Statute, the Chamber recognized that the 'Statute and the Rules reflect a growing recognition in international criminal law that there is a need to go beyond the

260 See Decision establishing the principles and procedures to be applied to reparations in the case of the *Prosecutor v. Thomas Lubanga Dyilo*, 7 August 2012, ICC-01/04-01/6 [hereinafter Reparations Decision].

261 Requests to appear before the Chamber and make submissions are made pursuant to Regulation 81(4) (b) of the Regulations of the Court on issues related to reparations.

The notion of punitive justice, towards a solution which is more inclusive.'262 This recognition is in keeping with established standards of international human rights law and particularly the 2005 UN Basic Principles. The Chamber took note of 2004 Report of the United Nations Secretary-General on the rule of law and transitional justice in conflict and post-conflict societies.263 The two main purposes for reparations according to the Chamber are that they oblige those responsible for crimes to repair the harm that they have caused and to enable the Chamber to ensure that offenders account for their acts.264

Within the context of transitional justice, the Chamber also recognized that reparations have the added advantage of promoting reconciliation between the convicted person, the victims of the crimes, and the affected communities. This statement has received conflicting reactions amongst transitional justice practitioners who are intimately aware of the situation in Ituri where the convicted person *Thomas Lubanga Dyilo* comes from. The conflict in Ituri, which the convicted person was a central part of, was one between the *Hema* and the *Lendu* communities. It is alleged that some of the children who joined the convicted person's rebellion, did so out of their own volition or were 'volunteered' by their parents and communities to fight the opposing group. Since the crimes that *Thomas Lubanga Dyilo* was convicted of involved the recruitment and use of children from his own community, the direct victims of the case in point and possibly direct beneficiaries of reparations are the child soldiers and their immediate families, from the convicted person's *Hema*

262 Reparations Decision, *supra* note 260, para 177.

263 Reparations Decision, *supra* note 260, footnote 367; See also The rule of law and transitional justice in conflict and post-conflict societies, Report of the United Nations Secretary-General s/2004/616, 23 August 2004; Updated Set of principles for the protection and promotion of human rights through action to combat impunity, Report of the independent expert Diane Orentlicher, E/CN.4/2005/102/Add.1, 8 February 2005

264 Reparations Decision, *supra* note 260, para 179;

community. The question is asked by the victims of the crimes committed by the child soldiers from the *Lendu* community as to how the reparations process would promote reconciliation between the two communities if the direct beneficiaries of the reparations will be the *Hema* community. These are some difficult situations presented in a post-conflict community and exacerbate the tension between the objectives of peace and justice.265 The Chamber has however noted that, for purposes of the application of principles of reparations under the Rome Statute, the Court will adopt a *broad and flexible* interpretation to give the *widest possible remedies* available to victims and evaluations on a case-by-case basis.266

The Chamber established the following principles:

a) Principle of Dignity, non-discrimination, and non-stigmatization – all victims regardless of their participation in the trial proceedings or not, will be treated fairly and equally.267 This principle may have the desired effect of curbing the increasing volumes of applications from victims to participate in proceedings at the Court discussed in an earlier section. This is the case where the principles are publicized effectively to victims and affected communities and reparations will take a non-discriminatory application.268

265 ICC Press Release, ICC-CPU-20121121-PR856 of 21 November 2012 'Katanga and Ngudjolo Chui case: ICC Trial Chamber II Severs Charges'...announces that the verdict in the case against Mathieu Ngudjolo will be issued on December 18, 2012. If he is found guilty of the crimes with which he is charged, there will be the possibility of reparation proceedings for purposes of addressing the harm caused to victims of his crimes. There is a wider

266 Reparations Decision, *supra* note 260, paras 180-181.

267 Reparations Decision, *supra* note 260, para 187

268 Reparations Decision, *supra* note 260, paras 258 and 259 where the Chamber pronounced that the responsibility of the publicity of the principles lies with the Registry and that its outreach activities with national authorities and local communities are encouraged.

b) Principles on Beneficiaries – the beneficiaries of reparations are both direct and indirect victims pursuant to Rule 85 RPE. As a direct victim may be clear, an indirect victim status may not be as clear. The Chamber will determine an indirect victim for example the parents of a child soldier.269 Legal entities may also benefit as victims but priority may be given to certain victims in vulnerable situations such as victims of sexual and gender-based violence.270

c) Principle on Accessibility and consultation with victims – the Chamber endorsed a gender-inclusive approach to all principles with sufficient consultations with victims *in situ* paying particular attention to their priorities.271

d) Principle on Victims of sexual violence – victims include women and girls, and boys and men alike. Reparations awards for this group of victims require a specialist, integrated and multidisciplinary approach particularly to meet obstacles faced by women and girls when seeking access to justice.272

e) Principle on Child victims – reparations decisions will be guided by the fundamental principle of the "best interests of the child" enshrined in the

Convention on the Rights of the Child. Where child soldiers are victims,

269 Reparations Decision, *supra* note 260, paras 194-195

270 Reparations Decision, *supra* note 260, paras 197-200.

271 Reparations Decision, *supra* note 260, paras 202-206.

272 Reparations Decision, *supra* note 260, paras. 207-209.

reparations programs must include their reintegration into society and rehabilitation to promote reconciliation within society.273

f) Principle on the Scope of reparations – the Chamber recognized the uncertainty in the number of victims in the case and despite the volumes of applications from victims, these numbers are not representatives of the totality of victims. The Chamber endorsed the use of both individual and collective reparations noting that the two are not mutually exclusive and may be awarded concurrently.274 When collective reparations are awarded, they should address the harm suffered by victims on an individual and collective basis.275

g) Principle on the Modalities of reparations – a comprehensive approach to reparations were adopted, including restitution, compensation (requires broad application consistent with international human rights law assessments of harm and damage), and rehabilitation. The Chamber reserved a non-exhaustive list of the forms of reparations not excluding those with symbolic, preventative, and transformative value.276

273 Reparations Decision, *supra* note 260, paras. 210-216.

274 Reparations Decision, *supra* note 260, paras. 217-220; See also Appeals Chamber Judgment on the The appeal of Mr. Thomas Lubanga Dyilo against the Decision on the defense Challenge to the Jurisdiction of the Court pursuant to Article 19(2)(a) of the Statute of 3 October 2006, 14 December 2006, ICC-01/04-01/06-772, para. 36.

275 Reparations Decision, *supra* note 260, para. 221.

276 Reparations Decision, *supra* note 260, paras. 222-241.

h) Principle on Proportional and adequate reparations – reparations should support programs that are self-sustaining and benefit aid by periodic installments rather than by way of lump-sum.277

i) Principle on Causation – the Court should not be limited to "direct" harm or the "immediate effects" of the crime, particularly in this case involving a child soldiers, but instead the Court should apply the standard of "proximate cause". The Court must be satisfied that there exists a "but/for" relationship between the crime and the harm.278

j) Principle on the Standard and Burden of Proof – as the trial stage is concluded when an order of reparations is considered, the appropriate standard of a balance of probabilities is sufficient. Where the reparations award emanates from the TFV a more flexible approach is to be taken.279 These kinds of awards are akin to what has become known as the second mandate operations and assistance of the TFV in situation countries of the Court outside of a judicial determination of guilt or innocence of an accused person.

In conclusion, the Chamber asserted the principle of respecting the rights of the defense in that nothing in the abovementioned principles will prejudice or be inconsistent with the rights of the convicted person to a fair and impartial trial.280

277 Reparations Decision, *supra* note 260, paras. 242-246.

278 Reparations Decision, *supra* note 260, paras 247-250.

279 Reparations Decision, *supra* note 260, paras. 251-254.

280 Reparations Decision, *supra* note 260, para. 255

1. Chapter IV

Enforcement Mechanisms to Secure International Cooperation

The need to continue codifying international law is apparent . . . But an even greater challenge for us now--and, in many respects an even greater opportunity--is enforcement. Although international law is often caricatured as elusive and abstract, there is nothing abstract about its enforcement . . . .

--Madeleine Albright281

4.1 INTRODUCTION

This chapter interrogates the enforcement mechanisms under the Rome Statute. Unlike States, the Court does not have an enforcement entity such as a Police Force

281 Albright MK, 'International Law Approaches the Twenty-First Century: A U.S. Perspectic Enforcement', (1995) *18 Fordham International Law Journal,* 1595, 1596

that would arrest persons accused of committing crimes within its jurisdiction, conduct searches and seizures or compel witnesses to appear before the Court. Yet, the Court must critically assess its practice of enforcing sentences that it imposes on convicted persons and in its contribution to restorative justice, the enforcement of reparations orders in collaboration with other Rome Statute entities such as the TFV.

The enforcement of sentences is an indispensable part of international criminal justice. In fact, it may be called the backbone of the system of international criminal justice.282 Even against this background, Kress, and Sluiter note that doctrinal writings on the enforcement of international criminal sentences are few yet critically needed to prepare for the enforcement regime of the Court.283 As with many other topics in international criminal law – including those discussed earlier in this thesis on the state cooperation in Chapter I, complementarity in Chapter II, the rights of persons at various stages of Court proceedings and processes in Chapter III – enforcement as governed by Part X of the Rome Statute read together with the relevant provisions of the RPE is the first elaborated codification and documentation of enforcement of international criminal sentences. At the time of this writing, the Court has rendered its first Judgment and Sentence against *Thomas Lubanga Dyilo*.284 In the same case, the Court has established the first-ever set of principles and procedures for the application of the reparations, regime etched in the Rome Statute.285 It is beneficial at this stage to reflect on the provisions for enforcement of sentences as well as of reparations orders by the Court with a view to contributing to the strengthening of the enforcement

282 Kress C & Sluiter G 'Preliminary Remarks' in the Rome Statute of the International Criminal Court: A Commentary Volume II (Cassese A, Gaeta P and Jones JRW eds) (Oxford: Oxford University Press, 2002), 1751-1756 [hereinafter Kress and Sluiter Preliminary Remarks], 1752

283 Kress and Sluiter Preliminary Remarks, *supra* note 282, 1755

284 Refer to the footnote in Chapter III on this decision

285 See Chapter III which analyses the principles and practices on the application of reparations under the Rome Statute

The regime of the Court and setting the point of departure for future Court determined sentences and reparations orders.

4.2 ENFORCEMENT OF SENTENCES UNDER THE ROME STATUTE

Part X of the Rome Statute clarifies that the enforcement relates to the regulations concerning the sentence that the Court has ordered for a convicted person as well as the enforcement of fines and forfeiture measures of the assets of a person who has been sentenced. There is an immediate connection between the enforcement of sentences with Part IX of the Rome Statute dealing with the cooperation of States with the Court. Article 103 elucidates the role of States in the enforcement of sentences of imprisonment. As mentioned previously, the Court does not have an enforcement agency and relies entirely on States to enforce sentences of imprisonment. States Parties are therefore acting in concert or in cooperation with the Court, in the enforcement regime under the Statute. Rule 199 RPE provides that 'the functions of the Court under Part 10 shall be exercised by the Presidency'.286 The Presidency287 shall designate a State drawn from a list of states maintained by the Registry288 in which a convicted person shall serve a sentence of imprisonment.289 In indicating their willingness and acceptance to enforce the sentences of imprisonment, States 'may attach conditions to its acceptance'290, which the Presidency is not obliged to accept but may request for additional clarity before making a decision to

286 Rule 199 RPE

287 The Presidency is one of four Organs of the Court established under Article 34 Rome Statute. According to Article 38 (3) '...the Presidency...shall be responsible for:

(a) The proper administration of the Court, with the exception of the Office of the Prosecutor; and

(b) The other functions conferred upon it in accordance with this Statute.'

288 According to Rule 200 (1) RPE, the Registry of the Court shall maintain a list of states which indicate their willingness to enforce a sentence of imprisonment for persons convicted by the Court.

289 Article 103 (1) (a) Rome Statute, *supra* note 1.

290 Article 103 (1) (b) Rome Statute, *supra* note 1.

include or exclude such a State from the list of states which will enforce sentences issued by the Court.291

The drafters of the Rome Statute in this Part maintained the sovereignty of states to determine what conditions in accordance with their national laws and procedures they would maintain in the enforcement of sentences. In the same breath, the drafters also wanted the Court to maintain a measure of control in the enforcement regime under the Statute. Every state has its unique laws and procedures of enforcement. Kress and Sluiter makes this distinct point that states '...distinguish the enforcement rules governing the question of *whether to enforce* from those governing the question of *how to enforce*.292 For some states the question of whether and how to enforce is governed by national criminal procedure legislation, while in others the two are treated separately and governed by different legislation.293 In an effort to harmonize the enforcement regime, the Court must then be seen as the ultimate overseer while maintaining state autonomy to determine conditions for enforcement. Article 106 (1) Rome Statute supports this position. It provides that,

"The enforcement of a sentence of imprisonment shall be subject to the supervision of the Court and shall be consistent with widely accepted international treaty standards governing the treatment of prisoners."

Article 106(1) introduces the concept of 'international treaty standards governing the treatment of prisoners' to the enforcement regime under the Rome Statute. These standards are traced to the Standard Minimum Rules for the Treatment of Prisoners

291 Rule 200 (2) RPE

292 Kress and Sluiter Preliminary Remarks, *supra* note 282, 1751

293 Kress and Sluiter Preliminary Remarks *supra* note 282, 1751 give the example of the United States where the law of corrections, which relates to *how to enforce,* is governed by the law of corrections,

which is entirely separate from the law of criminal procedure in the United States. adopted by the United Nations on 31 July 1957.294 These standard rules may be said to reflect customary international law.295 They were adopted at a time when the enforcement of prison sentences for convicted persons by the International Military Tribunal (IMT) at Nuremberg faced a measure of criticism. On 1 October 1946, the IMT at Nuremberg rendered its judgment on twenty-two major German war criminals. Three of the accused were acquitted.296 Of those convicted, the IMT at Nuremberg imposed twelve death sentences297, three terms of life imprisonment298, two terms of twenty years' imprisonment299, one term of fifteen years' imprisonment300, and one term of ten years imprisonment.301 The London Charter that established the IMT at Nuremberg did not provide for appellate proceedings following the trial stage. Once the judgment was issued, the enforcement stage followed. Article 29(1) of the London

The Charter provided the framework for enforcement. It states:

"In the case of guilt, sentences shall be carried out in accordance with the orders of the Allied Control Council for Germany, which may at any time reduce or otherwise alter the sentences, but may not increase the severity thereof."302

The Allied Control Council for Germany (ACCG) operated less on legal considerations than it did on political ones. The Council enforced prison sentences at the allied military prison at Berlin Spandau from 18 July 1947. The conditions of the

294 Standard Minimum Rules for the Treatment of Prisoners adopted by the United Nations on 31 July 1957 ECOSOC Res. 663 C (XXIV), amended by ECOSOC Res. 2076 (LXII), 13 May 1977

295 Rodley, N.S., *The Treatment of Prisoners under International Law* (1999) 278-279;

296 Fritzcshe, von Papen, and Schacht.

297 For Göring, Ribbentrop, Keitel, Kaltenbrunner, Rosenburg, Frank, Frick, Streicher, Sauckel, Johl, Seyß-Inquart and Bormann.

298 For Heß, Funk and Raeder.

299 For Schirach and Speer.

300 For Neurath.

301 For Dönitz.

302 Agreement for the Prosecution and Punishment of Major War Criminals of the European Axis, and Establishment of the Charter of the International Military Tribunal (IMT), 82 U.N.T.S. (1951) 279[hereinafter London Charter], Article 29(1).

imprisonment was said to be particularly hostile to the seven convicted persons. Although the rules at Spandau were eventually relaxed, it was clear that the objective of the allied powers in enforcing the sentences of the seven had very little to do with their rehabilitation.

The situation was not very different at the IMT in Tokyo. Section V of the Charter of the IMT for the Far East (IMTFE) set out the applicable penalties, as well as the method of enforcement. Article 17 on sentences reads

"...will be carried out in accordance with the Order of the Supreme Commander for the Allied Powers (SCAP), who may at any time reduce or otherwise alter the sentence, except to increase its severity."

Of the twenty-five accused, seven were sentenced to death303, sixteen to life imprisonment304, one to twenty years305, and one to seven years.306 Sentences were served at the Japanese prison of Sugamo in Tokyo.307 Unlike the enforcement regime of the IMT at Nuremberg, which was enforced by the four allied countries that of the IMTFE at Tokyo was enforced by Japan. In this sense, the IMT at Nuremberg represents a precedent for a multi-national enforcement regime. The conditions of imprisonment however was not very favorable to the prisoners, although there was a measure of grace according to the prisoners at Sugamo compared to those in Spandau.

303 Doihara, Hirota, Itagaki, Kimura, Matsui, Muto and Tojo.

304 Araki, Hashimoto, Hata, Hiranuma, Hoshino, Kaya, Kido, Koiso, Minami, Oka, Oshima, Sato, Shimada, Shiratori, Suzuki, and Umezu.

305 Togo.

306 Shigemitsu.

307 Kress C & Sluiter G 'Imprisonment' in the Rome Statute of the International Criminal Court: A Commentary Volume II (Cassese A, Gaeta P and Jones JRW eds) (Oxford: Oxford University Press, 2002), 1757-1821 [hereinafter Kress and Sluiter Imprisonment], 1762-4.

The striking similarity in both enforcement regimes however is the political considerations that went into decision-making at both ACCG and SCAP. Political sensitivities and considerations did not fade away in the debates at the UNSC following the genocide that took place in Rwanda in 1994, as did the IMT, IMFTE, and the enforcement institutions created thereunder. Rwanda, then a member of the UNSC voted against the Security Council Resolution 995 that established the ICTR, *inter alia*, on the ground that sentences of accused persons would be enforced in other countries but Rwanda and that the countries that will enforce the sentences would determine the nature of how the sentences will be carried out. Rwanda, dissatisfied with this position, argued that this must be 'for the International Tribunal or at least the Rwandese people to decide'.308

The designation of a State of enforcement following a conviction at the ICTR is governed by Article 26 ICTR Statute and Rule 103 ICTR RPE. The place of imprisonment from these provisions includes Rwanda.309 Article 27 of the ICTY Statute on the other hand does not specify what country the prison sentence shall be served save that a list of willing States will guide the relevant Chamber.

4.3 HORIZONTAL COOPERATION AMONG STATES ON ENFORCEMENT

308 UN Doc. S/PV.3453, 15 (1994)

309 Rule 103 (A) of the ICTR Rules of Procedure and Evidence reads as follows:

(A) Imprisonment shall be served in Rwanda or any State designated by the Tribunal from a list of States which have indicated their willingness to accept convicted persons for the serving of sentences. Prior to the decision on placement of imprisonment, the Chamber shall notify the Government of Rwanda.

From a completely utilitarian perspective, states have the common objective of preventing and suppressing criminality.310 There exists international cooperation among states on the enforcement of sentences of imprisonment. States are in the practice of concluding bilateral and multilateral agreements with each other to ensure that the objective of preventing and suppressing criminality is achieved.311 Abdul-Aziz posits that in these agreements, a State may wish that its nationals convicted abroad to complete their sentences in their national state.312 The views of the convicted person is weighed in the decision to transfer enforcement of prison terms.

Kress and Sluiter discuss two techniques employed by states in the enforcement of sentences. The first is the 'conversion' technique where a requesting state313 enforces the sentence and has the advantage of assuring itself that the trial resulting in the conviction was fair and that the penalty inflicted is not disproportionate. The second technique is one of 'continued enforcement' where the requesting state directly enforces and implements the sentence within the legal order of the requested state.314

4.4 VERTICAL COOPERATION AMONG STATES ON ENFORCEMENT

Vertical cooperation among states on the enforcement of prison sentences refers to the relationship and/or obligations of states with respect to the sentences ordered by the

310 Abdul-Aziz M, "Transfer of Prisoners: International Perspective", in M.C. Bassiouni (ed.), *International Criminal Law*, Vol. II. *Procedural and Enforcement Mechanisms* (2nd edn., 1999), 488 *et seq.* [hereinafter Abdul-Aziz]

311 Plachta M, *Transfer of Prisoners under International Instruments and Domestic Legislation* (1993)

143[hereinafter Plachta], identifies the agreement between Lebanon and Syria in 1951 as the first interstate

treaty on this point.

312 Abdul-Aziz, *supra* note 310, 250.

313 A requesting state is one where the convicted person will serve the sentence in imprisonment, often the state of nationality. The requested state is the state that conducts the trial of an accused and convicts.

314 Kress and Sluiter Imprisonment, *supra* note 307, 1767.

ICTY and ICTR. As previously mentioned, Article 27 ICTY Statute provides for the designation of a State that will enforce prison sentences. Rule 103 ICTY RPE and Practice Directions on the Procedure for the International Tribunal's Designation (Practice Directions) of the State in which a Convicted Person is to Serve his/her Sentence of Imprisonment guide the ICTY in this regard.315 Tolbert notes that in practice, there is no obligation on States to provide this form of cooperation with the ICTY or even the ICTR. States would have to be persuaded to provide the *ad hoc* Tribunals with assistance in this regard.316 Persuasion would take the form of requiring States to ensure that the domestic legislation meets the Tribunal's satisfaction of guarantees for the regulation of enforcement modalities. The *ad hoc* Tribunals would then sign an enforcement agreement with the particular State.317 Such agreements are guided by two principles that were established in the Sentence Judgment in the case of the *Prosecutor v. Drazen Erdemović*: respect for the duration of the penalty as imposed by the Chamber and respect for international rules governing the conditions of imprisonment.318 Kress and Sluiter emphasize that unlike the bilateral agreements between States that allow the concerns of the convicted person to be considered in the decision to effect the transfer of enforcement of the sentence, the ICTR and ICTY Statutes, RPE, Practice Directions, and case law do not indicate

315 Practice Directions on the Procedure for the International Tribunal's Designation were issued by the ICTY President on 9 July 1998.

316 Tolbert D, 'The International Tribunal for the former Yugoslavia and the Enforcement of Sentences', 11 *Leiden Journal of International Law* (1998) 655, 658.

317 Such agreements have been concluded between the ICTY and Austria, Bosnia and Herzegovina, Croatia, Denmark, Finland, France, Germany, Iran, Italy, Norway, Pakistan, Spain, and Sweden. Benin, Mali and Swaziland are the three African countries that have such an agreement with the ICTR. For the ICTR, the challenge, and criticism have been that the convicted persons should not serve their terms of imprisonment in the 'comfortable' prisons in Western countries. Many of the convicted persons by the ICTR remain in the UN Detention Facility at Arusha for a long period of time before being transferred to a State to serve their terms of imprisonment. Some of the convicted persons would complete their sentences at the UN Detention Facility.

318 Sentencing Judgment, *Prosecutor v. Drazen Erdemovič*, IT-96-22-T, 29 November 1996, para 34.

any duty for the President of the ICTY or ICTR to obtain the views of the convicted person on the designation of the State of enforcement.319

In as much as the *ad hoc* Tribunals provide a framework for vertical cooperation among states for the enforcement of sentencing, there are some outstanding issues that remain unresolved to date. Since the first convictions and sentencing in both *ad hoc* Tribunals, some of the convicted persons have since completed their terms of imprisonment but there has not been a standard mechanism to deal with their release into society. Some of the reasons for this include the unwillingness on the part of States to accept these individuals into their countries. It is often the case that the State of the nationality of the individual may not be safe or even willing to receive the individual. The Completion Strategies of the *ad hoc* Tribunals also do not pronounce much on the enforcement of sentences save for isolated cases.320 Nevertheless, the experiences of the *ad hoc* Tribunals will be of great persuasive value to the Court's

The presidency with respect to the enforcement of sentences.

4.5 COOPERATION OF STATES IN THE ENFORCEMENT OF SENTENCES UNDER THE ROME STATUTE

The ILC Draft Statute provided for a general obligation on the part of States to recognize and enforce judgments of the Court.321 This obligation to recognize would have meant that States parties to the Rome Statute had a direct obligation to cooperate

319 Kress & Sluiter Imprisonment, *supra* note 307, 1775

320Articles 12 of the Enforcement Agreements between the UN, Mali, and Benin concerning ICTR Sentences provide that, 'in the event that the Tribunal is to be wound up; the Registrar will inform the Security Council of any sentences whose enforcement remains to be completed pursuant to this agreement.'

321 Draft Statute of the International Law Commission UN Doc. A/49/10 [hereinafter ILC Draft Statute], Article 93(1)

with the Court to enforce sentences. The drafters of the Rome Statute had explicitly made room for the obligation to cooperate with the Court in its investigation and prosecution of crimes.322 Such an obligation to recognize and enforce Court judgments would possibly have dispensed with the Court's requirement to conclude specific agreements with States on enforcement, at least to the details of consent from the State as this is presumed from the signature and ratification of the Rome Statute as a whole and concomitantly with the obligation of States Parties to cooperate in this enforcement. There was no consensus among States in Rome concerning the provision on recognition and thus it was deleted from the final draft in Rome. States found a solution to the 'questions of how to determine the State of enforcement323, and how to ensure the supervision of the enforcement by the ICC324 and once it was decided how to deal with the issue of enforcement of fines and forfeiture orders325 exhaustively'326, which in their opinion dispensed with the need for a general clause obliging States to recognize the enforcement mechanism. There is therefore no general obligation on States Parties to cooperate with the Court in the enforcement of sentences of imprisonment in the Rome Statute. The same however cannot be said of enforcement of fines and forfeiture measures, which shall be discussed below.

4.5.1 Ensuring the cooperation of States in the enforcement of sentences of imprisonment

322 Article 86 Rome Statute, *supra* note 1; See also Chapter I which discusses the general obligation of States Parties to fully cooperate with the Court in its investigation and prosecution of crimes within its jurisdiction.

323 Articles 103 and 104 Rome Statute, *supra* note 1.

324 Articles 105 and 106 Rome Statute, *supra* note 1.

325 Article 109 Rome Statute, *supra* note 1.

326 Kress and Sluiter Imprisonment, *supra* note 307, 1786.

As explained above, a majority of the delegates at the Rome conference rejected an obligatory enforcement regime in the ILC Draft Statute in favor of the opt-in mechanism espoused in Article 103. Once a State on its own volition accepts to enforce the sentences of imprisonment and has been listed as such by the Court's Registry327, the Rome Statute gives the Court a measure of control over the enforcement mechanisms. Article 104 (1) reads that the 'Court may, at any time, decide to transfer a sentenced person to a prison of another State.' Article 105 also ensures that 'the Court alone shall have the right to decide and application for appeal and revision'. The supervisory power of the Court over the enforcement of sentences and conditions of imprisonment is made possible because of the permanent stature of the Court, unlike the *ad hoc* Tribunals. It is therefore possible for the Presidency to set up a mechanism to monitor and promote cooperation with States that opt to enforce prison sentences.

4.5.2 Ensuring the cooperation of States in the enforcement of fines and forfeitures

This form of enforcement is in comparison more sensitive to dealing with that prison sentences. For starters, in current Court practice, the enforcement is not applicable. Article 109 Rome Statute regulates the enforcement of fines and forfeiture measures. It reads

1. States Parties shall give effect to fines or forfeitures ordered by the Court under Part 7, without prejudice to the rights of bona fide third parties, and in accordance with the procedure of their national law

327 Rule 200 (1) RPE

2. If a State Party is unable to give effect to an order for forfeiture, it shall take measures to recover the value of the proceeds, property, or assets ordered by the Court to be forfeited, without prejudice to the rights of bona find third parties.

3. Property, or proceeds of the sale of real property or, where appropriate, the sale of other property, which is obtained by a State Party as a result of its enforcement of a judgment of the Court shall be transferred to the Court.

This article limits the enforcement of fines and forfeiture to those ordered by the Court under Article 77 (2) Rome Statute. The relevant portion provides that:

"...the Court may order:

(a) A fine under the criteria provided for in the Rules of Procedure and Evidence;

(b) A forfeiture of proceeds, property, and assets derived directly or indirectly from that crime, without prejudice to the rights of bona fide third parties."

Article 109 does not cover the fines imposed by the Court related to an offense against the administration of justice328 or provisional measures to secure evidentiary forfeiture.329 There is however a close relationship between the cooperation regime under Part IX of the Rome Statute and the enforcement of fines and forfeiture. From the language of the provision, States Parties are obliged to enforce fines and forfeiture orders. Rule 217 RPE elucidates that this obligation however does not automatically apply to States Parties, but rather that the Presidency must make a request to a State Party in accordance with Part IX of the Rome Statute dealing with cooperation.330 It

328 Article 70 (2) Rome Statute, *supra* note 1.

329 Article 93 (1) (k) Rome Statute, *supra* note 1.

330 Rule 271 RPE reads

remains however the prerogative of States Parties to give effect to fines or forfeiture orders in accordance with their national legislation governing such orders as expressed in Article 93 (1) (k) Rome Statute.

The Court has yet to enforce fines or forfeitures in the context of convicted persons. To date, only the Court has convicted one person, *Thomas Lubanga Dyilo*. At the commencement of the pre-trial phase, *Thomas Lubanga Dyilo* was declared indigent. In addition, the forfeiture of property relates to property that a convicted person acquired in the commission of the crimes s/he is convicted of. It is not immediately clear that the rebel group that *Thomas Lubanga Dyilo* led acquired the property during the conflict in Ituri, although it is not so far removed from an idea considering the mineral-rich eastern DRC. The challenge for the Court in this regard would be the identification of the assets of accused persons and here cooperation from States would support the process.

4.5.3 Ensuring the cooperation of States in the enforcement of reparations orders

Article 75(5) of the Rome Statute provides that 'a State Party shall give effect to a decision under this article as if the provision of article 109 were applicable to this article.' This reference suggests that there is separate enforcement of fines and forfeitures from the enforcement of reparations orders. In addition, the mandatory

For the enforcement of fines, forfeitures, or reparation orders, the Presidency shall, as appropriate, seek compensation and measures for enforcement in accordance with Part 9, as well as transmit copies of relevant orders to a State with the sentences the person appears to have direct connection by reason of wither nationality, domicile, or habitual residence or by virtue of the location of the sentenced person's assets and property or with which the victim has such a connection. The Presidency shall, as appropriate, inform the State of any third-party claims or the fact that no claim was presented by a person who received notification of any proceedings conducted pursuant to article 75.

language used in Article 75(5) places an obligatory enforcement regime on States Parties over reparations orders.

Kress and Sluiter advance that there is no practice of horizontal cooperation of states on the enforcement of reparations for victims of international crimes.331 The development of the reparations regime in international criminal justice has not been as fast as other components of international criminal law. The practice at the *ad hoc* Tribunals is limited in terms of enforcement of reparations orders. The enforcement of orders by the *ad hoc* Tribunals is limited to the return of stolen property or proceeds from the sale of such property.332 The obligation by States to enforce the orders of the *ad hoc* Tribunals is expressed in terms of the general duty to cooperate with the *ad hoc* Tribunals.333 In the case of the *Prosecutor v. Milošević et al.*, the ICTY ordered the provisional freezing of the assets of the accused following the Prosecutor's application under Rule 105 ICTY RPE for purposes of granting restitution.334 This order was transmitted to the UN Member States although there is no evidence of how vertical cooperation as described in Chapter I would have been executed by States in fulfillment of the ICTY's order.

4.6 CONCLUDING REMARKS

The Court has now established principles and practices for the application of reparations as discussed in Chapter III following the reparations order in the

331 Kress C & Sluiter G 'Fines and Forfeiture Orders' in the Rome Statute of the International Criminal Court: A Commentary Volume II (Cassese A, Gaeta P and Jones JRW eds) (Oxford: Oxford University Press, 2002), 1823-1848 [hereinafter Kress and Sluiter Fines and Forfeiture Orders], 1833

332 For example in Article 24(3) ICTY Statute

333 Article 29(1) ICTY Statute and

334 Decision on Review of Indictment and Application for Consequential Orders, *Prosecutor v. Slobodan Miloševič et al.*, 24 May 1999, IT-99-37, para. 27.

Prosecutor v. Thomas Lubanga case. The practice of awarding reparations for victims of international crimes has only just begun, while the debate on the national reparations programs for victims and affected communities of international crimes is steadily gaining traction. It will probably take some more time for inter-State practice on the enforcement of criminal law reparations orders to develop. The only precedent that exists for the enforcement of reparations orders is the case law of the ICTY. In the course of the negotiations on the enforcement of reparations orders under the Rome Statute, there was a proposal from the French delegation to include the attachment of an accused's property, assets, or money once an order under Article 75 Rome Statute had been made. This proposal was rejected on the grounds that delegations denied the existence of an obligation for States Parties to cooperate with the Court for purposes of adopting protective measures in the field of reparations.335

335 Kress and Sluiter Fines and Forfeiture Orders, *supra* note 49, 1834

5. CHAPTER V

Concluding Remarks

The Court is a permanent institution. In comparison to international law norms regulating the conduct of parties in hostilities and armed conflict, or those norms which govern the inalienable and 'non-derogate rights of an individual, the Rome Statutes establish new values and norms that have been in practice for a long period of time. Some of these norms have been assessed in this thesis under the general the rubric of cooperation of States generally336 and specifically in relation to complementary national jurisdictions,337 the rights of certain persons who appear before Court 338t338 and the enforcement of sentences and orders of the Court.339 The Rome Statute also codifies for the first time in a multilateral treaty, the prosecution of serious violations of the rules governing the conduct of parties in armed conflict considered as a part of customary international law. The origins of these relatively new norms of international criminal justice are therefore embedded in the 'tried and tested' norms in international humanitarian law and international human rights law.

When a critical reflection and assessment of the cooperation regime under the RoThe statuette is done, it is clear that there are several challenges that threaten to render the regime ineffective. It may be useful to provide some recommendations that identify opportunities to strengthen the cooperation regime established under Part IX of the Rome Statute.

336 See Chapter I on International Cooperation with the International Criminal Court.

337 See Chapter II on The Principle of Complementarity: Kenya's challenge of cooperating with the Court.

338 See Chapter III on The Rights of the Accused, Victims of International Crimes and Witnesses Appearing Before the Court.

339 See Chapter IV on Enforcement Mechanisms to Secure International Cooperation.

The structural weaknesses that characterize the system have been identified more so in the tenuous relationship between the Court, the AU, and the UNSC. As the two latter bodies function most from a political perspective, it may be important for the Court to assert its judicial functions by making pronouncements that regulate what seem to be contentious issues around cooperation. These pronouncements should buttress not only the general obligation of States Parties to cooperate fully with the Court but the specific aspects that would strengthen the domestic criminal jurisdictions to fulfill their treaty-based obligations. Perhaps there also is a need for a shift in focus from perceived neo-imperialist arguments advanced against the Court to the engine room of the Court to evaluate what does work and what does not work. In this connection, there should be a greater emphasis on the part of both the States Parties to the Rome Statute and the Court on the domestication of implementing legislation at the State–level to facilitate a robust and fully functional international cooperation regime.

The UNSC plays an important role as one of the trigger mechanisms for investigation and prosecution by the Court in terms of Articles 13(b), 15 *ter,* and 16 of the Rome Statute. As the Court is still in its infancy stage and need of legitimacy especially in States that are aggrieved by its *modus operandi* in the first ten years since the Court began its work, will need the institutional support of the UNSC. Whereas reform of the UN is outside the scope of this thesis, the UNSC as it is currently constituted must exercise its Chapter VII powers given to it by the Charter of the UN to maintain regional peace and security to the exclusion of political considerations that undermine the Courts functions. As non-permanent members of the UNSC as it is currently constituted are selected from different regions of the world, the UNSC may want to pay particular emphasis on a consultative process with regional representatives where a situation merits the attention of the Court. It may also be beneficial to invite representatives of a situation under UNSC consideration to the deliberations of UNSC action relating to the Court. Coincidentally, Rwanda was a non-permanent member of the UNSC from 1994 to 1995 when deliberations concerning the establishment of the ICTR took place following the genocide in that country in 1994. The views and concerns of the concerned State, whether a Party or non-State Party of the Rome Statute and other actors such as civil society organizations working in the situation under UNSC consideration may positively influence UNSC decision-making relating to its Rome Statute powers. These consultative processes have the capacity to promote effective cooperation between States and the Court when the jurisdiction of the Court is invoked in a country that has been referred by the UNSC.

Regional integration bodies *inter alia*: the AU, the European Union ("EU") and the The organization of the American States ("OAS") has a role to play to strengthen the Court. There already exists an international mechanism to deal with the investigations and prosecutions of war crimes, crimes against humanity, and genocide through the auspices of the Rome Statute, specifically created as a treaty entity by the community of States. It is counter-productive to the suppression of these crimes and the objects of justice for victims when regional integration bodies embark on the creation of new supranational courts akin to the existing Court, whatever the reasons may be. More than 160 governments participated in the conference that adopted the Rome Statute. This number represents more than two-thirds of the nations on earth. In the negotiations for a permanent international criminal court, not once is it recorded that States preferred to establish or endow regional courts with international criminal jurisdiction. Rather, States were interested in enhancing national as well as the Court's capacity to deal with these heinous crimes. Regional bodies may however support the Court's cooperation regime by advocating for the universalization of the Rome Statute and focus energies on accession to the Rome Statute for their member States who are not Party to the Rome Statute. In addition, regional bodies, especially the AU should conclude cooperation agreements with the Court that would delineate specific roles and responsibilities of both the Court and the regional body under the the shared objective of fighting against impunity.

The enhancement of national criminal jurisdictions to deal with international crimes is A key process that States should embark on. The real intention of the 160 governments represented in Rome prior to the adoption of the Rome Statute was that their sovereignty to deal with their nationals who are alleged to have committed war crimes, crimes against humanity and genocide remains intact. As discussed in Chapter II, it is in the interests of all States, whether Party or non-Party to the Rome Statute to have criminal justice systems that would address these crimes in a genuine fashion. Where any given State finds a lacuna in its national legislation incapacitating it from dealing with international crimes, it must seek to immediately remedy such a situation. The responsibility to build the capacity of such states is however not the sole responsibility of the individual State. The principle of positive complementarity envisages that other States as well as the Court can build the capacity of States to investigate and prosecute international crimes. The Court, its staff, and its growing jurisprudence have thematic expertise that would be useful in strengthening national criminal justice systems. This form of cooperation only serves to strengthen States to fight against impunity for international crimes as well as deal with specific thematic issues such as the protection of witnesses and victims that are key for the work of national criminal justice systems.

National criminal justice systems that are strengthened would be able to respond to requests for the enforcement of Court sentences and orders. As it is clear that there is no general obligation on States Parties to enforce the Court's sentences, the Court relies on States for the enforcement. In fact, the solution to many of the Court's challenges lie in the strengthening of national criminal justice systems. The Court remains the last resort to deal with international crimes and to redress victims of these crimes. The concept of localized trials should be extended to the reparations regime. Although this was not addressed in detail in this thesis, strengthened national criminal justice systems include the extension of States' capacity to deal with the right to reparations at the national level. Ideally, such capacity would also assist in the enforcement of Court ordered reparations.

A relationship of cooperation between the Court and States Parties is the lifeline of the Court and more importantly the legitimization of the international criminal justice system. It will take the concerted efforts of States to develop the international justice system and put into practice the theory behind the system – the enforcement of a a rules-based system that protects children, women, and men from atrocities that deeply shock the conscience of humanity.

List of Cases

International Court of Justice

Barcelona Traction case [Belgium v. Spain] (Second Phase) ICJ Rep 1970 3

Case Concerning the Arrest Warrant of 11 April 2000 (Democratic Republic of Congo v Belgium) ICJ 14 Feb 2002; 41 ILM 536 (2002)

International Criminal Court

Prosecutor v Katanga and Chui ICC-01/04-01/07-1497

Prosecutor v Muthaura, Kenyatta and Ali ICC-01.09-02/11-274

Prosecutor v. Omar Hassan Ahmad Al Bashir, ICC-02/05-01/09, 27

Prosecutor v Ruto, Kosgey and Sang, ICC-01/09-01/11-307

Prosecutor v. Thomas Lubanga Dyilo, Case No.: ICC-01/04-01/06, Trial Chamber,

International Criminal Tribunal for the former Yugoslavia

Prosecutor v. Drazen Erdemovič, IT-96-22-T

Prosecutor v. Krstić, Case No. IT-98-33-A

Prosecutor v. Milosevic, Case No. IT-02-54, 9

Prosecutor v. Tihomir Blaskić, Case No.: IT-95-14-AR108 bis

South Africa

Mohamed and Another v. President of the Republic of South Africa and Others 2001 (3) SA 893 (CC)

Thatcher v Minister of Justice and Constitutional Development & Others 2005 (4) SA 543 (C)

List of Treaties

African Charter on Human and Peoples' Rights, June 27, 1981, 21 ILM 59

Agreement for the Prosecution and Punishment of Major War Criminals of the European Axis, and Establishment of the Charter of the International Military Tribunal (IMT), 82 U.N.T.S. (1951) 279

American Convention on Human Rights, Nov. 22, 1969, 9 I.L.M. 673

Basic Principles and Guidelines on the Right to a Remedy and Reparations for Victims of Gross Violations of International Human Rights Law and Serious Violations of International Humanitarian Law, GA Res., UNGAOR, 60th Sess., UN Doc. A/Res/60/147 (16 December 2005)

Charter of the International Military Tribunal, Aug 18, 1945, 59 Stat. 1544, 82 U.N.T.S. 279

Charter of the United Nations, 24 October 1945, 1 UNTS XVI

Convention against Torture and Other Cruel, Inhuman or Degrading Treatment or Punishment, U.N. GAOR, 39th Sess., Supp. No. 51, at 197, U.N. Doc. A/39/51 (1984)

Draft Statute of the International Law Commission UN Doc. A/49/10

European Convention for the Protection of Human Rights and Fundamental Freedoms, Nov. 4, 1950, 312 U.N.T.S. 221, E.T.S. 5, as amended by Protocol No. 3, E.T.S. 45, Protocol No. 5, E.T.S. 55, and Protocol No. 8, E.T.S. 118

Geneva Convention for the Amelioration of the Condition of the Wounded and Sick in Armed Forces in the Field, Oct. 21, 1950, 75 U.N.T.S. 31

Geneva Convention for the Amelioration of the Condition of Wounded, Sick and

Shipwrecked Members of Armed Forces at Sea, Oct. 21, 1950, 75 U.N.T.S. 85

Geneva Convention Relative to the Treatment of Prisoners of War, Oct. 21, 1950, 75 U.N.T.S. 135

Geneva Convention Relative to the Protection of Civilian Persons in Time of War, Oct. 21, 1950, 75 U.N.T.S. 287

International Covenant on Civil and Political Rights, Dec. 16, 1966, 999 U.N.T.S. 171

Protocol Additional to the Geneva Conventions of 12 August 1949, and Relating to the Protection of Victims of International Armed Conflicts, Dec. 7, 1978, 1125 U.N.T.S. 3

Protocol Additional to the Geneva Conventions of 12 August 1949, and Relating to the Protection of Victims of Non-International Armed Conflicts, Dec. 7, 1978, 1125 U.N.T.S. 609

Protocol to the African Charter on Human and Peoples' Rights on the Establishment of an African Court on Human and Peoples' Rights

Rome Statute of the International Criminal Court UN Doc A/CONF. 183/9; 37 ILM 1002 (1998); 2187 UNTS 90

Standard Minimum Rules for the Treatment of Prisoners adopted by the United Nations on 31 July 1957 ECOSOC Res. 663 C (XXIV), amended by ECOSOC Res. 2076 (LXII), 13 May 1977

Statute of the International Tribunal for the former Yugoslavia (1993) Security council Resolution 827 (1993) on Establishing an International Tribunal for the Prosecution of Persons Responsible for Serious Violations of International Humanitarian law Committed in the Territory of the Former Yugoslavia, (1993) *ILM* 1192; as amended by Security Council Resolution 1166 of 13 May 1998

Statute of the International Criminal Tribunal for Rwanda (1994) Security Council Resolution 955 Establishing the Prosecution of Persons Responsible for Genocide and

Other Serious Violations of International Humanitarian Law Committed in the The territory of Rwanda and Rwandan Citizens responsible for genocide and other such violations committed in the territory of neighboring States, between 1 January 1994 and 31 December 1994

Universal Declaration of Human Rights, G.A. Res. 217, U.N. GAOR, 3d Sess., at 72, U.N. Doc. A/810 (1948)

Vienna Convention on the Law of Treaties

List of United Nations Resolutions

United Nations Security Council Resolution 808 (1993) of 22 February 1993

United Nations Security Council Resolution 955 (1994) of 8 November 1994

List of National Legislation

Amnesty Act 2000 of the Laws of Uganda

Commissions of Inquiry Act, Cap 102 Laws of Kenya, Commission for the Investigation of Post-Election Violence, Kenya Gazette Notice No. 4473 and 4474 of 23 May 2008

Constitution of Kenya, 2010

Bibliography

Articles in Journals

Albright MK, 'International Law Approaches the Twenty-First Century: The U.S. Perspective on Enforcement', (1995) *18 Fordham International Law Journal,* 1595

Aldana-Pindell, 'In vindication of justiciable victims' right to truth and justice for state-sponsored crimes' 35*Vanderbilt Journal of Transnational Law* 1399-1501

Arsanjani, M.H, 'The Rome Statute of the International Criminal Court', *American Journal of International Law* (1999) 22-69

Bassiouni, M.C, 'The Right to Restitution, Compensation, and Rehabilitation for Victims of Gross Violations of Human Rights and Fundamental Freedoms' (2000)

UNESCOR, 56th Sess. UN Doc. E/CN.4/2000/62

Benzing M., *The Complementarity Regime of the International Criminal Court: International Criminal Justice between State Sovereignty and the Fight Against Impunity*, 7 Max Plank Yearbook of United Nations Law 591, at 601

Cassese, A 'On the Current Trends towards Criminal Prosecution and Punishment of Breaches of International Humanitarian Law' 9 EJIL (1998) 1, at 13

Chung "Victims' Participation at the International Criminal Court: Are concessions of the Court clouding the promise" 2008 6 *Northwestern University Journal of Human Rights* 159-227

Du Plessis, Max 'The *Thatcher* case and the supposed delicacies of foreign affairs: a plea for a principled (and realistic) approach to the duty of government to ensure that South Africans abroad are not exposed to the death penalty 2 *South African Journal of Criminal Justice* (2007) 143-157

Haslam E, 'Victim Participation at the International Criminal Court: A triumph of hope over experience?' in D. McGoldrick, P Rowe & E Donnely, The Permanent International Criminal Court: Legal and Policies Issues (2004) 315-334

Hathaway OA, "Between Power and Principle: An integrated Theory of International Law" 71 *University of Chicago Law Review* (2005) 1

Henzelin M, Heiskanen V & Mettraux G, 'Reparations to Victims Before the International Criminal Court: Lessons from international mass claims processes (2006) 17 *Criminal Law Forum* 317-344

Inazumi, Mitsue 'The Meaning of the State Consent Precondition in Article 12(2) of the Rome Statute of the International Criminal Court: a theoretical analysis of the source of international criminal jurisdiction' 49 *Netherlands International Law Review* (2002) 159-193

Jurdi Nidal, "Some Lessons on Complementarity for the International Criminal Court

Review Conference", 34 South African Yearbook of International Law (2009) 28

Kemp, Gerhard 'Foreign Relations, International Co-operation in Criminal Matters and the position of the Individual' 16 (3) *South African Journal on Criminal Justice* (2003) 368-392

Kemp, Gerhard 'The United Nations Convention Against Transnational Organized Crime: A milestone in international criminal law' 2 *South African Journal of Criminal Justice* (2001) 152-167

Kim, Young Sok 'The Cooperation of a State to Establish an Effective Permanent International Criminal Court' *Journal of International Law & Practice* 6 (1997) 157-173.

Koskenniemi 'International law in Europe: Between tradition and renewal' (2005) 16 *European Journal of International Law* 113

Mekjian GJ and Varughese MC 'Hearing the Victims' Voice: Analysis of victims' advocate participation in the trial proceeding of the International Criminal Court 2005 XVII 1 *Pace University School of Law Journal* 1-49

McGoldrick, Dominic 'The Permanent International Court: an end to the culture of impunity?' *Criminal Law Report* (1999) 627-655

Roht-Arriaza N, 'Reparations Decisions and Dilemmas' (2004) 27 *Hastings International and Comparative Law Review,* 157-219

Saul B 'Compensation for Unlawful Death in International Law: A focus on the Inter-American Court of Human Rights (2004) 19 *American University International Law Review* 523-584

Seguin, J. "Denouncing the International Criminal Court: An Examination of U.S. Objections to the Rome Statute", *18 Boston University International Law Journal* (2000), 99-100

Shelton D, 'Righting Wrongs: Reparations in the Articles of State Responsibility' 96

American Journal of International Law (2002), 833-856

Stahn C, 'Complementarity, Amnesties and Alternative Forms of Justice: Some interpretive guidelines for the International Criminal Court (2005) *Journal of International Criminal Justice*, 695 – 716

Stapleton S, 'Ensuring a Fair Trial in the International Criminal Court: Statutory interpretation and the impermissibility of derogation' (1999) 31 *New York University Journal of International Law and Politics*, 535-592

Tladi D, "The African Union and the International Criminal Court: The battle for the soul of international law" 34 *South African Yearbook of International Law* (2009), 57 -69

Tolbert D, 'The International Tribunal for the former Yugoslavia and the Enforcement of Sentences', 11 *Leiden Journal of International Law* (1998) 655

Van Boven T, 'Study Concerning the right to Restitution, Compensation and Rehabilitation for Victims of Gross Violations of Human Rights and Fundamental Freedoms' UN Doc E/CN.4/Sub.2/1993/8 of 2 July 1993

Van den Wyngaert "Victims Before International Criminal Courts: Some views and concerns of an ICC Trial Judge" 2011 44 *Case Western Reserve Journal of International Law* 475-493

Watson GR "The Passive Personality Principle" 28 *Texas International Law Journal* 1 (1993)

[1] 1 Rome Statute of the International Criminal Court UN Doc A/CONF. 183/9; 37 ILM 1002 (1998);

2 A. Ciampi, The Obligation to Cooperate, in *Reflections on the International Criminal Court: Essays in Honour of Adriaan Bos*, edited by H.A.M. Von Hebel, J.G. Lammers and J. Schukking (1998)(OUP), 1607 -1638, at 1607-8

3 See Statute of the International Tribunal for the former Yugoslavia (1993) Security Council Resolution 827 (1993) on Establishing an International Tribunal for the Prosecution of Persons Responsible for Serious Violations of International Humanitarian law Committed in the Territory of the

Former Yugoslavia, (1993) *ILM* 1192; as amended by Security Council Resolution 1166 of 13 May 1998, available at http://www.un.org/icty/ [accessed 5 February 2010]. Statute of the International Criminal Tribunal for Rwanda (1994) Security Council Resolution 955 Establishing the Prosecution of Persons Responsible for Genocide and Other Serious Violations of International Humanitarian Law Committed in the Territory of Rwanda and Rwandan Citizens responsible for genocide and other such violations committed in the territory of neighbouring States, between 1 January 1994 and 31 December 1994, available at http://www.un.org/ictr [accessed 5 February 2010]

4 United Nations, *Charter of the United Nations*, 24 October 1945, 1 UNTS XVI:

[2] 5 Obligations *erga omnes* are obligations recognized in international law as owed by States towards the community of States as a whole. See *Barcelona Traction case* [Belgium v. Spain] (Second Phase) ICJ Rep 1970 3 par 33 "...an essential distinction should be drawn between the obligations of a State towards the international community as a whole, and those arising vis-à-vis another State in the field of diplomatic protection. By their very nature, the former are the concern of all States. In view of the importance of the rights involved, all States can be held to have a legal interest in their protection; they are obligations *erga omnes*. [at 34] Such obligations derive, for example, in contemporary international law, from the outlawing of acts of aggression, and of genocide, as also from the principles and rules concerning the basic rights of the human person, including protection from slavery and racial discrimination."

6 The Rome Statute as an international treaty only binds States which are parties to it. This is in accordance with a well-established principle of international law. For a restatement of this rule, see Art. 34 of the Vienna Convention on the Law of Treaties: '*A treaty does not create either obligations or rights for a third State without its consent*'

7 A. Ciampi, *supra* note 2, at 1608

8 Art. 13 (b) Rome Statute, *supra* note 1

[3] 9 Calvo-Guller K. N, *The Trial Proceedings of the International Criminal Court* (2006) (MartinusNijhoff) at 17.

10 See "Decision on Sentence Pursuant to Article 76", *The Prosecutor v. Thomas Lubanga Dyilo*, Case No.: ICC-01/04-01/06, Trial Chamber, 10 July 2012, paras. 88-91.

11 *See* "Judgement on the Request of the Republic of Croatia for Review of the Decision of Trial Chamber II of 18 July 1997", *The Prosecutor v. Tihomir Blaskić,* Case No.: IT-95-14-AR108 *bis,* Appeals Chamber, 29 October 1997, para. 26.

12 B Swart, General Problems. In *Reflections on the International Criminal Court: Essays in Honour of Adriaan Bos*, edited by H.A.M. Von Hebel, J.G. Lammers and J. Schukking, 1589

13 A Cassese, 'On the Current Trends towards Criminal Prosecution and Punishment of Breaches of International Humanitarian Law' 9 EJIL (1998) 1, at 13

[4]

[5]

[6] 14 A State's jurisdiction refers to the competence of the State to govern persons and property by its criminal and civil law.

15 Active personality jurisdiction exercised by court based on the nationality of the perpetrator of the crime whereas passive personality jurisdiction is exercised by the courts of the nationality of the victim of the crime; *See* Watson GR "The Passive Personality Principle" 28 *Texas International Law Journal* 1 (1993) and Hathaway OA, "Between Power and Principle: An integrated Theory of International Law" 71 *University of Chicago Law Review* (2005) 1, where the active personality and passive personality principles of jurisdiction are defined and explained.

[7] 17 *Supra* note 3; *See also* United Nations Security Council Resolution 808 (1993) of 22 February 1993 established an international tribunal for the prosecution of persons responsible for the serious violations of international humanitarian law committed in the territory of the former Yugoslavia since 1991 with its seat in The Hague available at http://www.icty.org/x/file/Legal%20Library/Statute/statute_808_1993_en.pdf [accessed 3 October 2012].

18 *Supra* note 3; *See also* United Nations Security Council Resolution 955 (1994) of 8 November 1994

established an international tribunal for the prosecution of persons responsible for genocide and other serious violations of international humanitarian law committee din the territory of Rwanda between 1 January1994 and 31 December 1994 with its seat in Arusha available at http://www.unictr.org/Portals/0/English/Legal/Resolutions/English/955e.pdf [accessed 3 October 2012].

19 *Prosecutor v. Timohir Blaškić*, Appeals Chamber, 29 October 1997, IT-99-14-AR 108*bis*, para. 47 and 54.

20 Henckaerts J. and Doswald-Beck L., *Customary International Humanitarian Law, Volume I: Rules*, (2005) (Cambridge University Press), xvi

[8]21 See Rebecca M.M. Wallace *International Law* 5th (2009) 20.

22 As at the time of this writing, there are 121 States that have ratified the Rome Statute. The Rome Statute does not have universal application at this time, although there are campaigns by civil society organizations in the world for universalism.

23 The following countries participated in the negotiations between States prior to the adoption of the Rome Statute, and appended their signatures to the treaty: Egypt, India, Russia and the United States of America – which has since declared that it has withdrawn its signature from the treaty.

[9]25 Article 87 Rome Statute *supra* note 1.

26 Article 87 (1) (b) Rome Statute *supra* note 1.

27 Article 2 Rome Statute *supra* note 1 reads that:

The Court shall be brought into relationship with the United Nations through an agreement to be approved by the Assembly of State Parties to this Statute and thereafter concluded by the President of the Court on its behalf.

This agreement between the two inter-governmental organizations has been concluded.

[10]

[11]31 Most recently, news reports that the Attorney General of Kenya received a letter from the Head of Jurisdiction, Complementarity and Cooperation in the ICC Prosecutor's Office complaining of tardy

responses from Kenya in the ongoing investigations and soon-to-commence trials of four Kenyans at the ICC. The Attorney General maintained that Kenya is committed to the Rome Statute regime. *See* All Africa article "Kenya: Githu Passes the Buck Over ICC" available at http://allafrica.com/stories/201210020046.html [accessed 5 October 2012].

28 Article 87 (5) (b) Rome Statute *supra* note 1. It is interesting to note that although the general rule is that treaties do not create obligations or rights for third parties in accordance with Article 36 of the Vienna Convention on the Law of Treaties, the drafters of the Rome Statute were aware that prior to the universalisation of the Rome Statute, there is a need to have 'catch all' provisions in the Rome Statute to ensure that the true spirit of creating a permanent international criminal court to deal with crimes of a serious nature, are not impeded by technicalities in international law. The mechanisms of the United Nations Security Council are employed in this manner.

29 Decision informing the United Nations Security Council and the Assembly of the States Parties to the Rome Statute about Omar Al-Bashir's presence in the territory of the Republic of Kenya, *Prosecutor v. Omar Hassan Ahmad Al Bashir,* ICC-02/05-01/09, 27 August 2010.

30 Article 87 (4) Rome Statute *supra* note 1.

[12]32 Article 87 (5) (a) Rome Statute *supra* note 1.

[13]33 At the time of this writing, 33 African states are party to the Rome Statute.

34 As at the time of this writing the following African countries have implementing legislation at either draft stage or enacted laws (domesticating) with cooperation and complementarity provisions: Benin, Botswana, Burundi, Congo (Republic of), Central African Republic, Democratic Republic of Congo, Gabon, Ghana, Kenya, Lesotho, Mali, Niger, Nigeria, Senegal and South Africa. *See* "Amnesty International: The ICC Summary of draft and enacted complementing legislation as at April 2006" available at http://www.iccnow.org/documents/AI_Implementation_factsheet06Nov14.pdf [accessed 5 October 2012].

[14]39 Swart (supra) 1589.

40 See ICC Press Release, President of Uganda Refers Situation Concerning the Lord's Resistance

Army (LRA) to the ICC (Jan. 29, 2004); See ICC Press Release, Prosecutor of the International Criminal Court Opens Investigation into Northern Uganda (July 29, 2004).

41 See ICC Press Release, Prosecutor Receives Referral of the Situation in the Democratic Republic of Congo (Apr. 19, 2004); See ICC Press Release, The Office of the Prosecutor of the International Criminal Court Opens its First Investigation (June 23, 2004).

42 See ICC Press Release ICC-OTP-20050107-86, Prosecutor Receives Referral of the Situation in the Central African Republic (July 7, 2005); See ICC Press Release ICC-OTP-20070522-220, the Office of the Prosecutor of the International Criminal Court Opens its Investigation in CAR (May 22, 2007).

[15]43 There is an outstanding warrant for the arrest of *Bosco Ntaganda*, leader of a rebel group operating in the east of the DRC. Reports by civil society indicate that the suspect resides in eastern DRC in plain view of the authorities but continues to enjoy free movement.

44 The Pre-Trial Chamber of the ICC has issued warrants for the arrest of *Joseph Kony, Vincent Otti, Okot Odhiambo, Dominic Ongwen, Raska Lukwiya (deceased)*. The four suspects are at large and suspected to be in hiding in Garamba National Park in eastern DRC, the Central African Republic or in South Sudan.

[16]45 Article 13 (b) Rome Statute; Chapter VII of the UN Charter deals with the provisions relating to exercise of powers by the UNSC for the maintenance of international peace and security where a threat to the peace has occurred.

46 Article 25 UN Charter provides that "*The Members of the United Nations agree to accept and carry out the decisions of the Security Council in accordance with the present Charter.*"

[17]

[18]52 Addressing African heads of State at the 15th AU Summit in Kampala, the Vice President of Botswana said "Botswana cannot associate herself with any decision which calls upon her to disregard her obligations to the International Criminal Court." Available at http://www.gov.bw/en/News/Botswana-stands-by-the-International-Criminal-Court-/ (accessed July 19, 2011); See Statement by the Botswana Ministry of Foreign Affairs and International Cooperation

following 17th AU Heads of State Summit in Malabo, Equatorial Guinea calling African States Parties to the Rome Statute not to cooperate with the ICC in effecting Gaddafi's arrest warrant. "The Government of Botswana pledges to continue to uphold basic human and political rights and hereby calls on fellow members of the AU to support the ICC in carrying out its mandate to apprehend the Libyan leader, as a critical step towards alleviating the plights of the Libyan people, and having the way for a new democratic dispensation in that country." Available at http://www.mofaic.gov.bw/index.php (accessed July 19, 2011)

53 *See* "Zambia ready to arrest Al Bashir" which appeared in The Sunday Times of Malawi, available at http://www.bnltimes.com/index.php/sunday-times/headlines/national/6528-zambia-ready-to-arrest-albashir

[Accessed 3/10/2012].

54 Tladi D, "The African Union and the International Criminal Court: The battle for the soul of international law" 34 *South African Yearbook of International Law* (2009), 57 -69, 57-58

[19]130 See International Covenant on Civil and Political Rights, Dec. 16, 1966, 999 U.N.T.S. 171 [hereinafter ICCPR], Articles 9, 14, & 15; the African Charter on Human and Peoples' Rights, June 27, 1981,21 I.L.M 59 [hereinafter African Charter], Articles 3, 6, & 7; American Convention on Human Rights, Nov. 22, 1969, 9 I.L.M. 673 [hereinafter ACHR], Articles 7, 8, & 9; European Convention for the Protection of Human Rights and Fundamental Freedoms, Nov. 4, 1950, 312 U.N.T.S. 221, E.T.S. 5, as amended by Protocol No. 3, E.T.S. 45, Protocol No. 5, E.T.S. 55, and Protocol No. 8, E.T.S. 118 [hereinafter ECHR], Articles. 5, 6, & 7; Geneva Convention for the Amelioration of the Condition of the Wounded and Sick in Armed Forces in the Field, Oct. 21, 1950, 75 U.N.T.S. 31[hereinafter GCI], Article 3; Geneva Convention for the Amelioration of the Condition of Wounded, Sick and Shipwrecked Members of Armed Forces at Sea, Oct. 21, 1950, 75 U.N.T.S. 85 [hereinafter GCII], Article 3; Geneva Convention Relative to the Treatment of Prisoners of War, Oct. 21, 1950, 75 U.N.T.S. 135 [hereinafter GCIII], Article 3; Geneva Convention Relative to the Protection of Civilian Persons in Time of War, Oct. 21, 1950, 75 U.N.T.S. 287 [hereinafter GCIV], Article 3; Protocol

[20]Additional to the Geneva Conventions of 12 August 1949, and Relating to the Protection of Victims of International Armed Conflicts, Dec. 7, 1978, 1125 U.N.T.S. 3 [hereinafter Additional Protocol I], Article 75 (Fundamental Guarantees); Protocol Additional to the Geneva Conventions of 12 August 1949, and Relating to the Protection of Victims of Non-International Armed Conflicts, Dec. 7, 1978, 1125 U.N.T.S. 609 [hereinafter Additional Protocol II], Article 6 (Penal Prosecutions); Convention against Torture and Other Cruel, Inhuman or Degrading Treatment or Punishment, U.N. GAOR, 39th Sess., Supp. No. 51, at 197, U.N. Doc. A/39/51 (1984), Article 7; Universal Declaration of Human Rights, G.A. Res. 217, U.N. GAOR, 3d Sess., at 72, U.N. Doc. A/810 (1948) [hereinafter UDHR], Articles 9-11.

131 Stapleton S, 'Ensuring a Fair Trial in the International Criminal Court: Statutory interpretation and the impermissibility of derogation' (1999) 31 *New York University Journal of International Law and Politics*, 535-592, 535.

132 Stapleton, *supra* note 131

133 See provisions of human rights treaties *supra* note 130.

[21]134 Compare Article 16 of the Charter of the International Military Tribunal, Aug 18, 1945, 59 Stat. 1544, 82 U.N.T.S. 279, which provides that

In order to ensure fair trial for the defendants, the following procedure shall be followed: (a) The Indictment.... (b) During any preliminary examination or trial of a Defendant he shall have the right to give any explanation relevant to the charges made against him. (c) A preliminary examination.... (d) A Defendant shall have the right to conduct his own defense before the Tribunal or to have the assistance of Counsel. (e) A defendant shall have the right through himself or through his Counsel to present evidence at the Trial in support of his defense, and to cross examine any witness called by the Prosecution.

with Article 21 ICTY Statute, *supra* note 3 and Article 20 ICTR Statute, *supra* note 3 which both

Contents

Printed by Libri Plureos GmbH in Hamburg,
Germany